Description in Philosophy

Description in Philosophy

With a particular reference to
Wittgenstein and Husserl

Krishna Jain

DK
PRINTWORLD
Publishers of Indian Traditions

Cataloging in Publication Data – DK
[Courtesy: D.K. Agencies (P) Ltd. <docinfo@dkagencies.com>]

Jain, Krishna, 1947.
Description in philosophy.
Includes bibliographical references (p.).
Includes index
ISBN 9788124600260

1. Wittgenstein, Ludwig, 1889-1951 – Criticism and interpretation. 2. Husserl, Edmund, 1859-1938 – Criticism and interpretation 3. Description (Philosophy).
I. Title

ISBN: 978-81-246-0026-0
First published in India in 1994
Second impression 2018

Printed and published by:
D.K. Printworld (P) Ltd.
Regd. Office: "Vedaśrī", F-395, Sudarshan Park
(Metro Station: ESI Hospital), New Delhi - 110 015
Phones: (011) 2545 3975; 2546 6019
e-mail: indology@dkprintworld.com
Website: www.dkprintworld.com

To

Siddharth, my son,
who is still trying to
unravel the mysteries
of language

Preface

THE word 'description' had always been haunting the twentieth century philosophers. The first clear use of it is found in Russell's works, although he was not a descriptive philosopher. Descartes, Locke and Kant in the seventeenth and eighteenth centuries, were non-descriptive philosophers and were primarily concerned with the validity of claims to know. Their interest centred around the 'foundation' of knowledge. Their faith in the notion of philosophy as a foundational discipline, however, resulted in constructing systems.

Husserl and Wittgenstein broke off from the traditional attitude towards philosophy. They introduced 'new maps of the terrain' by initiating new ways of looking at it. Their attempt was not to "ground" this or "criticize" that but to describe what "lies before us". They presented no ideology or systems or theories but aspired to describe what one sees. They believed that philosophy was overloaded with jargons and theories and felt there was a need to simplify it. They considered it a ritual which was to be performed by philosophers, and took upon themselves the humble task of description in philosophy. Pre-historic world and primitive society have been seen by them as an indispensable soil bed without which philosophical description is not possible. Philosophy in their works turns towards what is original, natural and native.

The descriptive philosophy is not dependent on some assumed "*a priori*" constraint. It is first person's rather than third person's inquiry of the surrounding. Descriptive philosophy, one could say, is "therapeutic" rather than "constructive". The focus in philosophical description is on the analysis of language and experience. It may be perceived as a methodology having two aspects, viz pure seeing (seeing without prejudice) and its expression in language. But a gap between them is inevitable as the language cannot capture all human experiences in its net and pure description will always, therefore, remain a myth.

We are concerned here not with the impossibility of philosophical description but with the hazards which inevitably arise in the way of faithful description and with the idea of faithful description itself. We are also not concerned with the similarities and dissimilarities between Wittgenstein's analytical philosophy and Husserl's phenomenology but with the manner they pursued the concept of descriptive philosophy in their own philosophical set up.

Philosophical description as a method practised by them requires a certain framework, a certain 'matrix' which make description possible. Without some anchorage like forms of life or life world, philosophical description would be utterly devoid of philosophical import. Wittgenstein and Husserl although depart from the classical world views in their descriptive programme, yet they both, in the last analysis, abandon description. The piecemeal strategies with which they started are eventually swallowed up, not in speculation, but in the matrix which gave them birth. In a sense this matrix in spite of being indispensable, sets the limit for description.

It is my pleasant duty to express profound regards and gratitude to Dr. (Mrs.) Margaret Chatterjee, formerly Professor and Head of the Department of philosophy, Delhi University who as my research supervisor was a source of constant help and encouragement. I am indebted to Dr. (Mrs.) S. Jain, my teacher and former Principal of Janki Devi College who inculcated in me the desire to indulge in research activities. I am also grateful to Major B.K. Singh and his wife Suchita for their help in preparing the press copy. Finally, I don't have adequate words to express what I owe to my husband Dr. V.K. Jain without whose cooperation and assistance it would not have been possible to complete the present work.

Krishna Jain

Contents

1

The Concept of Description

DESCRIPTION in philosophy started primarily as a reaction against speculative systems. Speculative metaphysics claims to be concerned with ultimate reality, the thing–in–itself as opposed to appearance. But in modern times interest has shifted from ontology to epistemology, from 'What there is' to 'What is given'. Some philosophers started reflecting on what is 'given' in our experience rather than on something which may be beyond appearance.

In speculative philosophy there was always an assumption of an order of things on which experience and language depended. Josiah Royce said that traditional philosophers had thought of just "one true order of things"[1] and that led to the construction of closed systems. The interest of classical philosophers was in the *existence* of reality rather than with its meaning. Along with this went a particular style of philosophizing. The classical philosophers did not claim to be doing descriptions. They were creative thinkers and their interest was in the construction of philosophical systems. Description, on the other hand, is a piecemeal method of elucidation and clarification. Philosophers who were interested in descriptive philosophy regarded the practice of system-building in philosophy almost as a sin. Not only ancient philosophers but some modern philosophers also went in for system-making. The systems of modern rationalists like those of Descartes, Spinoza, Leibniz, however, were mathematical. That is to say they sought the help of 'pure science' in devising their own methodology. Nevertheless, the aim of both of ancient and modern speculative philosophers was primarily theoretical. Descartes was impressed by the Galilean certainty of a universal yet material world which is a "being-in-itself" and can only be known mathematically in its pure essence. The other rationalists were equally influenced by the new scientific discoveries and the prestige that the latter had. Consequently, philosophy in the seventeenth century was dominated by uncompromising mathematical systems. Descartes found in the *Cogito* the fundamental basis for knowledge. Though he proposed a radical philosophical method yet he was a traditionalist in so far as he provided a *system*. He put natural phenomena into a mathematical framework. But the factual situations refuse to obey a fixed pattern.

Descriptive philosophy gives up the project of making overall theories and turn to piecemeal investigations. This philosophy does not claim to provide knowledge of something *new* but supposed to be doing something totally *different*. A descriptive philosopher is satisfied with the elementary data i.e. with basic bricks which are 'given' to him. He does not aspire to construct theories or systems out of them. Description, one can say, is a kind of *ritual* which is performed by certain twentieth century philosophers in order to clarify philosophical puzzles. The search is not for system or theories. Descriptive philosophy is primarily concerned with the thing "lying before us" i.e. with what is evident. Philosophy becomes "prima philosophia" in the sense that the interest of such philosophers is in the phenomena as they appear, instead of discussing how it exists, still less *if* it exists.

The objects of philosophical description are not deduced or inferred, they are 'given'. An important question arises in this context "What are the objects of philosophical description?" One can say that the objects of philosophical description are to be distinguished from the objects of ordinary description in virtue of their 'mode of givenness'. The objects of ordinary description are 'given' to the physical senses, but objects of philosophical description are not given in this way. Nor are the objects of philosophical description *a priori,* for that would lead to speculative philosophy. It may not be wrong to say that the objects of philosophical description are 'given' through the peculiar faculty of 'intuition'. That is perhaps why J.N. Mohanty says, "philosophical description stands or falls with the idea of intuition."[2] This is, however, not clearly stated by any other philosopher except Husserl. Moreover, the objects of philosophical description inevitably and necessarily reveal a profound field of philosophical inquiry, whereas the objects of ordinary description have no such implications. This is at least one important difference between philosophical and non-philosophical description.

It was the empiricists in the seventeenth century who for the first time stressed the importance of the 'given'. They emphasized sense experience against mystical or dogmatic thinking (which are, of course, not the same thing). British empiricism was virtually a revolt against the philosophical departure from the common sense view. Distrust of philosophical systems can be said to date from Locke's descriptive method. He proposed "to follow what he calls a "historical plain method" by which he meant a simple description of the facts relevant to the subject matter of his inquiry".[3] The old fashioned use of the word 'historical' here is intended to convey the sense of description. Locke gave a factual account of the functioning of mind in its relation to objects. This was an immensely powerful weapon against obscurantism and dogmatism and it gave a new direction to European philosophy and also provided a new basis for the science of psychology.

Locke's descriptive method overlaps with the critical method. He criticised the rationalists, especially Descartes, for discarding the use of empirical language for philosophical purposes. At the end of Book II of the *Essay,* Locke found it necessary to examine the "nature, use and signification" of language, for he thought there is a close connection between words and ideas, particularly between abstract ideas and general words. For Locke the primary functions of language are to communicate with fellow men. Words stand as marks for ideas. "Words, in their primary or immediate signification, stand for nothing but *the ideas in the mind of him that uses them* ....."[4] The language which is emphasized here is not artificial but empirical. For Locke, empirical language is not different from philosophical language. There is, for him, no such thing as a special "philosophical language." This emphasis on empirical language by empiricists and by Locke in particular, was the first step in the direction of descriptive philosophy. On such a view a mathematically-loaded language is incompatible with philosophical *discourse.*

Moreover, knowledge based on mathematics is demonstrative whereas knowledge about "reality" cannot be demonstrative. Sensible knowledge is non-demonstrative and hence non-mathematical. Locke, for the first time clearly distinguished demonstrative from non-demonstrative knowledge. The recognition of knowledge about the sensible world as non-demonstrative was yet another stepping stone along the path of descriptive philosophy.

Furthermore Locke's discussion of description is associated with what he conceives the 'unit' of knowledge to be, i.e., with the simple idea and its origin. Since ideas are caused by material objects, the analysis of knowledge in Locke assumes a causal form. It follows a model drawn from chemistry. The notion of 'units' of description was continued by some later descriptive philosophers also but not by all.

It is true descriptive philosophy started with Locke, but is must be noted that his description was psychological rather than philosophical. Moreover, Locke's philosophy is attached to a particular kind of psychology based on an atomistic approach. The process of the development of mind is regarded as a genetic process. He was concerned with the actual functioning of the human mind. It was for this reason that Kant speaks of Locke's epistemology as an anatomy of knowledge.

After Locke the most outstanding example of psychological description is that which is given by Hume. In describing the origin of ideas and the functioning of the mind Hume follows Locke, but he draws the empiricist direction of Locke to its furthest limit. He removed all possible "metaphysical ghosts" from philosophy. Methodologically Hume is a non-speculative philosopher par excellence. For him epistemology is more or less equivalent to psychology.

Hume's policy both in the *Treatise* and in the *Enquiry* was to apply the Newtonian experimental method to investigations into the powers and principles of the human mind. The intended result was to be a truly experimental science of human nature. But the crucial criticism Hume faces, as in the case of Locke, is that his treatment is genetic rather than analytic. He deals with how understanding *occurs* rather than with what understanding *is,* still less with what it is for an expression to have a meaning. The stress on the origin of ideas amounts to positive geneticism and is of little use for a descriptive philosophy. Moreover, Hume's epistemological theory was based on a model taken from mechanics to which he was committed from the beginning. That is why the description he gives has been called 'pesudo-description'.[5]

Turning to Kant whose work was *critical* in a full-fledged sense we must frankly grant that his aim was not descriptive at all. He does not *describe* experiences but brings to light the conditions which make description possible. He points out that the very description of possible experiences presupposes certain necessary conditions which no philosophy of experience can afford to overlook. The question "what is necessarily true of the world that we experience" is illuminatingly approached by asking "what are the general conditions of any possible employment of our human faculties?" Kant is thus concerned with the *a priori* framework which *enables description.* This *a priori* framework consists of human cognative functions which make us see things as they appear. In this way Kant's critical philosophy provides a new type of reasoning which is adjusted to the task of linking experience to the non-empirical. Not concerned with the task of constructing a metaphysical system of "First Principles", Kant's critical philosophy is preoccupied with the major problems of establishing a necessary link between the empirical and the non-empirical. Out of this stems his famous formula, "All our knowledge begins with experience but does not arise out of experience." This, however, amounts to transcendental philosophy, and not to a philosophy of the transcendent.

The word 'description', one could say, has haunted the twentieth century philosophy. The analysis of the problem of description is strictly speaking found only in this century. Two great movements of our time, analytical philosophy and phenomenology assign to philosophy the task of description. The interest of both of them is centred around 'meaning'. Both are concerned with how things (whether phenomena or locations) show themselves. Interest shifts to what is presented to us rather than to either psychological or metaphysical questions. The *analysis* of phenomena becomes important although phenomena, of course, have different meanings for each. Analytical philosophers are interested in linguistic phenomena whereas phenomenologists deal with pure essences.

For neither is philosophical description psychological. The new empiricism emphasized the neutrality of sense data. In order to fight against psychology Russell, Wittgenstein and other philosophers of an empiricist temper brought in symbolic logic, artificially constructed ideal language, truth-functional devices and other highly sophisticated mathematical and logical techniques all designed to serve the general goal of neutrality. Psychological analysis was replaced by logical analysis. The importance of the mind was granted but in a neutralised way. Ryle's *Concept of Mind* is the leading example of this. The human mind is not regarded as an entity or process or class of events radically distinct from corporeal events or things but, on the contrary, very generally speaking, seen in a functional way.

Phenomenologists no less than linguistic analysts fight against the use of psychology in philosophy. But instead of taking the help of logic and mathematics (although Husserl arrived at his new method by a study of these), Husserl, the founder of phenomenology, developed an entirely new method. The transcendental phenomenological method was designed to get rid of psychologism. The transcendental method replaces 'descriptive psychology' by 'descriptive phenomenology'. The first volume of *Logical Investigations* to a greater extent, and *Philosophy as Rigorous Science* to a lesser extent are, to all intents and purposes, critiques of psychologism.

Psychology for Husserl is a positive science, a science of mental events and facts. Phenomenology, on the other hand, purports to be a science not of facts but of "essential being", of "essences". It deals with what is *a priori* in the sense of depending on no extraneous thing for its 'matter'. Psychology cannot give more than empirical generalization. It cannot yield what is apodictically evident. Even the objective validity of laws in the natural sciences, Husserl argues, cannot be derived merely from inductive generalization. Such validity rests ultimately on the ideal possibility of an adequate consciousness of universal or "general evidence" as Husserl would put it.

For a psychologist, consciousness is a natural phenomenon, while for Husserl consciousness is an autonomous region of pure experiences. In psychology, mental phenomena are understood in terms of their causes, while phenomenologists analyse objectivity in terms of the structures of intentionality of consciousness. For Husserl psychologism arises primarily from a deep-seated tendency to confuse intended structures, structures of consciousness, with particular psychological acts of consciousness. He departed from Brentano perhaps because the latter is psychologistic.

Both analytical philosophy and phenomenology arose, on the one hand, out of dissatisfaction with speculative philosophy and, on the other, with dissatisfaction with psychological analysis. Philosophers dealing with description are concerned with a phenomenal level which is yet distinct from fact. It is science, not philosophy, that is concerned with facts. The logical analysis that belongs to analytical philosophy is independent of whatever may be discovered empirically. Similarly phenomenology stresses its independence from the positive science.

It is not for philosophy to give information about reality or to describe natural operations. Its business is to analyse the general forms of propositions which are quite independent of whatever may be discovered empirically. Both phenomenology as well analytical philosophy wish to analyse the logical meanings of thought apart from circumstances of facts which are studied by sciences like psychology and neurology. In fact, they make an attempt to arrive at a methodological investigation that is not directed to empirical objects (those being left to sciences) but to the propositions employed by scientific and other uses of language. For Husserl "meaning" is a matter of content and for Wittgenstein it is more a matter of form.

The question may arise what are the essential features or similarities of philosophical description? The philosophical description is, in fact, neither psychological nor genetic. It is also neither to reduce nor to speculate; it is not to hypothesize either. To describe is not to construct or reconstruct interpretative frameworks and models. Its aim is to give no theories, no systems, no 'ism', no school. Description is not reporting either. Wittgenstein makes a distinction between *berichten* (reporting) and *beschreiben* (description). For whereas the former is true or false, the latter has no such evaluative notion.

The concept of description is actually aimed at philosophizing without any presupposition, prejudice, prejudgement and absolutization. A truly descriptive philosophy does not commit itself to any ontology or metaphysics; it is rather ontology which needs description. The question now arises, how to find out whether a description is pure or it carries preconceptions with it? In order to expose the pretentious character of a pseudo-description we must always put the following question : Does it contain any ontological, metaphysical, religious or epistemological presupposition? If it does, it is not a descriptive philosophy. Description is a method, a form of philosophizing, an activity, a speech act. It tries to answer questions like what is/what is like rather than what is/was it? Describing means to witness something.[6]

All philosophers interested in description as a methodology are describing structural aspects of our understanding. While Wittgenstein emphasizes that a logical structure can sometimes be disclosed merely by the analysis of what is already given objectively in the element and rules of language, Husserl, in the very same case, emphasizes the identifying and synthesizing activity of the subject in such a disclosure of structure. The structures are not simply there; they are at work, they become visible.

The problem of description in philosophy was introduced by the linguistic philosophers in two ways. One way of considering description in philosophy was to focus on philosophical language from the point of view of seeing it as the gateway to reality. The structure of language reveals the structure of "what is". The interest in philosophical language arises only because it is a means to this. In the early twentieth century it was a fashion to look on language as external to reality, something which we employ propositionally to 'reflect' reality.[7] Russell, and earlier Wittgenstein introduced the problem of description in this particular context. In the latter phase of his work Husserl was certainly very conscious of the peculiar role that language has in revealing objects and of the peculiarity of linguistic objects themselves. This, however, does not mean that Russell, the earlier Wittgenstein and Husserl were doing similar things. Their philosophical methods are poles apart. The conception of 'what is' is different in each case although in each case it is somehow or the other tied up with language. The other way in which the linguistic analytical philosophers stressed description in philosophy was to *criticize* philosophical language. Some linguistic philosophers analyzed philosophical language which was traditionally used by the philosophers. They analyzed with a view to detecting wrong uses of language. But Oxford philosophers and the later Wittgenstein turned to the description of the nature and functioning of *empirical* language for it was this that provided the yardstick of correct usage for them.

The first clear use of the word 'description', however, in twentieth century philosophy is found in Russell's works. Russell's main interests were in the foundations of mathematics and the analysis of perceptual knowledge. He assumes that the introduction of the scientific method in philosophy is the proper thing for a philosopher to do. Russell confines himself to the meanings of words and sentences. In order that a sentence should be meaningful, however, it is not necessary that it should refer to existent objects. He criticised Meinong, the Austrian philosopher, who assigned a metasphysical status to all substantive terms. In abandoning Meinong's doctrine, Russell adopts the device of *analysis* of statements containing unreal or self-contradictory objects, an analysis which would both preserve our robust sense of reality and still allow us to talk intelligibly about such "pseudo-objects". Clarification plays a key role in Russell's philosophy, whereas it was ontology that dominated Meinong's discussions. The treatment of description in Russell was tied up with his rejection of ontology. But whether he was able to carry this through becomes doubtful by the time we come to his logical atomistic phase. Russell does not rule out all ontology. He rejects only the ontology of transcendent entities. He takes his stand on sense data. Like Descartes, Russell is trapped into the conviction that there is something absolutely simple and certain from where the philosopher can begin. Material objects like chairs and tables are logical constructions out of sense data and not inferred from them. Russell eleminates inference to transcendent entities, whereas inferring to such entities had been the essential characteristic of speculative philosophy.

Knowledge of material objects, however, is 'by des-cription', whereas knowledge of sense data is 'by acquaintance'. But Russell later on grants that knowledge, whether it is immediate or mediate is not the product of experience alone. It necessarily requires postulates.[8] Though Russell begins as a thorough going empiricist, he eventually grants the importance of postulates in the constitution of human knowledge in his later work and concedes their indispensability.

Analysis, no doubt, plays a key role in Russell's work. He says logic is the essence of philosophy. Now it is important to see what type of analysis Russell practised, for the discussion of description in Russell is closely tied up with this. The analysis of language in Russell is done on the analogy of the analysis of logical and mathematical language. For Russell only an ideal language constructed on the analogy of mathematical language can be properly regarded as philosophical language. Ordinary language, he found, is full of metaphors and analogies and hence it cannot be a philosophical language. Because of this Russell was labelled as an ideal language philosopher. Ordinary grammar too is utterly confusing and is the source of philosophical problems. Not only Meinong, but all the traditional philosophers were misled by ordinary grammar. Colloquial language is fine as long as it serves practical purposes but for philosophy it is not adequate. In place of 'ordinary grammar' Russell purposes 'logical grammar' which is constituted of symbols and variables only. A faultless and ideal language is constructed on the pattern of mathematics. The language of *Principia Mathematica* is intended to be a model language. It is a symbolic and truth-functional language. All the binary operations of mathematics play an important role in constructing this new language. Thus Russell's discussion of description presupposes a model, a mathematical model. While the model in Locke was causal, in Russell the model is derived from mathematics. His philosophy of description is, however, essentially logical and not mathematical. The critics can say that a philosophy governed by models cannot describe things as they are, only as they appear in the light of the presupposed models.

Russell's treatment of description may be said to be that of a simplified description, for he reduces material things to sense data in the interest of clarification. His descriptions are like scientific descriptions in an important sense, for both use constructive analysis of a reductive type. In science there is stress on "micro-reduction" whereby the macro-properties of an object are explained by reference to its micro-properties.

Scientific discussions are descriptive as well as explanatory. Scientific laws explain natural phenomena. For example, material objects are described in terms of atoms by scientists. Russell too talked about atoms but they are neither physical nor mental but logical. This is why Russell called his philosophy 'logical atomism'.

Later phenomenalism also claims to be descriptive. The emphasis here is on the meaningful use of language. But only the language of a sense data is recognised to be meaningful. It provides the core meaning for empirical discussion. Material object language was translated into sense datum language. The former was reduced to the latter, the claim being that thereby no loss of meaning was involved. Russell's translation of ordinary language into the language of constructions claimed to provide conceptual clarification. It was in fact a tool of philosophical analysis.

But what we find in phenomenalism (of the reductivist kind) is a recommendation of an artificial process of translation. It is carried on with the help of mathematical and logical devices. Like Russell, the later phenomenalists also think that empirical language cannot be philosophical language. Therefore they create a new language. It may not be irrelevant to ask why they should have accepted the language of sense data as the only meaningful language. It is because they think only sense data are directly 'given' and are thus free from prejudices, theories and contradictory interpretations. They are fascinated by the general 'myth of neutrality' of sense data. J.N. Mohanty in an article read at the Delhi Philosophical Colloquium says that philosophers both ancient as well as modern are obsessed with the notion of 'givenness' because acceptance of some such thing provides absolute certainty to their philosophy.[9] The phenomenalists are no exception to this. Moreover, it seems that phenomenalists were governed by the conviction that by 'given' we necessarily mean what is to be accepted passively. For them any description which starts with reflective thought is classified as a 'pseudo description'. Against this it could be maintained of both the 'given' and the field of philosophical inquiry that neither are known entirely passively. One has to rise up to a level of reflective philosophical thinking in order to describe philosophically. The 'given' is by no means the uncritically accepted. To determine the field of philosophical inquiry is "a critical procedure; it cannot *just* be descriptive".[10] A.J. Ayer, a prominent phenomenalist (although these days he has modified his phenomenalism considerably) admits that "Sometimes it is enough to have them (facts) simply pointed out to us, but often reasons must be supplied for thinking that a given description of them is correct".[11] Moreover, "the concept of *translation* --- is closely akin to what is often termed "interpretation".[12]

So philosophical description is neither reductive analysis *á la* Russell nor the causal "plain" method of the early empiricists. In a sense although Russell provides a "philosophy of description" he does not adhere actually to a programme of philosophical description himself. For the latter is concerned primarily with the use of ordinary language for philosophical purposes whereas Russell is dealing with the use of ideal language in order to give a philosophy of description.

Now there are two other groups of philosophers ordinary language philosophers (those who think ordinary language can be used for philosophical purposes) and phenomenologists who claim to be using a descriptive method. Both of them, however, are doing different types of description in different fields with different backgrounds. The Oxford philosophers like Ryle, Austin, Strawson and also Wittgenstein provide analytical description of everyday language. They examine the "unexplored fertility of natural language", and believe that there is no need to construct a new language for ordinary language is "all right" for philosophical purposes. So they look upon their descriptive philosophy, in fact, as a reaction to "ideal" language. The idea of a perfect and artificial language in philosophy did not, however, start with Russell. Descartes for the first time talked about the 'universal language' and even more so, Leibniz felt the need for a calculus, a universal language for philosophical discussion. It has only syntax and no vocabulary whatsoever. One of the main purposes of constructing an ideal language in the twentieth century was to provide a framework for the picture theory. Along with the invention of a symbolic language runs the conviction that language must correspond to facts. Wittgenstein's *Tractatus* is the leading example of this. Description here takes the form of depiction. However, Wittgenstein abandoned his programme of depiction later on although he retained the idea of description and gave a new twist to it. As far as the formation of artificial languages is concerned, they did not serve the purpose for which they were intended because ordinary language resists truth-functional, interpretation. Ordinary language is very different indeed from artificial language. For this reason neither can throw light on the other nor can either serve as a model for the other.

In view of what we have said so far we might suppose that it is not ideal language but ordinary language which is useful for descriptive philosophy. Descriptive philosophy describes faithfully what is "seen" directly. For this, ordinary language is adequate. A philosophy centred on description is not isolated from its socio-cultural background and this includes the fact that there is a multiplicity of languages. An ideal language which is set in a single mould cannot serve us here. Natural languages (as distinct from artificial calculi) have multiple uses. There are various ways in which one can "do things with words". Philosophers, or at least those who follow a linguistic programme, analyse and describe the various uses of language. Their slogan becomes "Let the use of words teach you their meaning",[13] or "Don't ask for meanings ask for the use".[14] and if the meanings of words are to be defined in use, then we have to admit that use is in constant process of revision.

To the analytical philosophers language is 'given' as phenomenon and it is tied up with actual communication.[15] Language is given to grammarians also and they also describe language. But for them language is a natural phenomenon. For philosophers, the importance of language arises from the fact that every philosophical problem is related to it. Philosophical questions are raised and discussed through language.

Use is, however, different from usage. 'Use' is lan guage-neutral, while usage 'is language specific'.[16] For instance, if we enquire about the *usage* of 'table', then we are concerned with how that particular English word is employed by those who employ it and not with the common characteristics of a table. If we enquire about the *use* of 'table', then we are simultaneously and equally concerned with the use of the term in other languages also, e.g. like 'tavola'.[17] Ordinary language philosophers are concerned only with the language neutral conditions that govern the use to which a particular piece of language could be put. Description of uses of language does not 'interfere' with the actual workings of language.[18] A philosopher is concerned with the concept of "table". For linguistic philosophers, philosophy deals only with conceptual analysis. They distinguish philosophy from linguistic studies but at the same time emphasize that concepts are nonetheless expressed only through language. Hence for Wittgenstein what is really needed is a clarification of our everyday thinking, and experimental investigations are of no help in this task. Only more careful conceptual analysis can do the trick.

The phenomenologists, on the other hand, deal with what is directly 'given' to us in pure intuition. The task of the phenomenologist is to describe what is 'seen' and not to construct theories or systems. Instead of language, however, phenomenologists are concerned with the region of consciousness. This is 'given' to psychologists also, but for them consciousness is a natural phenomenon. As against this the primacy of the realm of consciousness in phenomenology arises from the consideration that everything is 'seen' through consciousness. This contrast reveals that consciousness, as treated in non-philosophical description, is a given natural fact, whereas for philosophical description consciousness constitutes the "essences". It is with this new field that phenomenology deals.

The aim of phenomenologists is to describe this new field. Husserl says, "we have defended the claims of pure description ---".[19] Heidegger even goes further and says "The expression 'descriptive phenomenology' . . . is at bottom tautological ....".[20] But Heidegger seems to be wrong here for there are phenomenologies which are not descriptive. Hegel's phenomenology, for instance, is not descriptive. In his first major work *Phenomenology of the Spirit,* Hegel's primary aim is to provide the Absolute System of Spirit (Mind). His *Phenomenology* traced the development of Spirit through various stages, in which it apprehends itself as phenomenon, to the point of full development where it is aware of itself as it is in itself - as noumenon. For Hegal phenomenology is the science in which we come to know mind as it is in itself through the study of the ways in which it appears to us. Hegel's task is to reach the noumenal realm. The actual nature of Spirit (or Mind) is hidden behind its appearances.

The feature of Hegel's phenomenology that might seem to bring it close to the descriptive phenomenology of Husserl is that it too deals with phenomenon or "appearances" or, more specifically, with the appearances of Spirit i.e. its *manifestations* in which it appears "for itself". But at this point we have to be on our guard against a fundamental and rather fateful equivocation of the word "appearances". Hegel's appearances of the Spirit constitute stages in the development or history of consciousness; in this sense he is concerned with an ontological problem and the appearances are nothing but progressive realisations of the ideal of "scientific consciousness". In contrast, Husserl deals with those "appearances" which are the slanted views through which an identical thing makes its appearance, as it occurs particularly in perception. These appearances of Husserl differ fundamentally from the Hegelian appearances which are not transparent vis-a-vis something appearing through them. The Hegelian "appearances" are primarily an expression of a developing entity in reality, and definitely not the way in which an object is 'given' through its appearances. His interest was not in describing what lies before us but to construct an Absolute system of Spirit. Moreover, knowledge of Absolute Mind was not acquired through the descriptive method but through the dialectical method. Hegel's phenomenology is thus dialectical and not descriptive.

Heidegger's phenomenology too is not descriptive. In *Sein Und Zeit,* he defended hermeneutic phenomenology against Husserl's descriptive phenomenology. Although in the same work Heidegger claims that phenomenology is by nature descriptive, but immediately after this declaration he says "the meaning of phenomenological description as a method lies in *interpretation*".[21]

The philosopher's task is to return "to the things themselves" in contrast to all unsupported constructions and theories. But the thing for Heidegger, is not fully 'given'. Instead, being, the pure phenomenon, is 'hidden', 'covered up', and "shows itself 'in disguise'". The pure phenomenon does *not* show itself but remains hidden as the meaning and ground of what shows itself, yet at the same time it belongs to it so essentially as to constitute its meaning and its ground.

Without interpretation Being cannot be fully manifested. The phenomenon calls for much more than merely direct seeing. In this way Heideggar's phenomenology certainly goes beyond the immediately 'given' if immediacy means mainfest 'givenness'. It requires anticipations which go beyond it, and requires extrapolation beyond what is directly present. So phenomenology, for Heidegger, becomes the method of uncovering the hidden, or the "interpretation" *(Auslogung)* of the hidden. As against descriptive philosophy simpliciter Heidegger thinks that precisely because the phenomena are for the most part *not* given, the need for phenomenology arises. Covered-up-ness is the counter concept to that of 'phenomenon'. The primary phenomenon which needs uncovering in this sense is Being, the victim of our usual forgetfulness of the ontological difference between Being and the thing-in-itself, (where the latter is seen as counterposed to phenomena).

But what exactly is the new interpretation which Heidegger's phenomenological ontology demands? It is in this connection that the term "hermeneutic" appears in Heidegger's phenomenology. The term "hermeneutic" no longer refers to documents or symbolic expressions but to non-sumbolic facts of the real world, to the human being or *Dasein.* Just as consciousness is defined as 'consciousness of' by Husserl, the human being is characterised by Heidegger as being in the world. This is why Heidegger is labelled as an existentialist. Instead of bracketing the existential world like Husserl, Heidegger realised the importance of it for revealing phenomena. Being is interpreted in terms of the everyday world. In fact it is for the interpretation of this particular type of being that Heidegger reserves the term "hermeneutic". Phenomenology, for Heidegger, thus is the theme of ontology.

Other existentialists too who, in spite of dealing with direct inner experiences, are yet not strictly descriptive. The inner experiences are expressed in a 'confessional' tone. An existentialist is interested in 'witnessing to' his individual experiences. His expression of individual experiences, however, does not result always in clear and distinct perceptions by any means but in distinct intimations and recollections, the very stuff of 'confessional writings', to be found in journals, diaries and the like, literary genres in which the existentialists were to excel.[22] The existentislist prefers an indirect mode of expression - fiction presented in the form of a novel or drama, private journals and other forms of writing in which are to be found echoes of the personal life. The existentialist is not satisfied with a return to things themselves by direct intuition. He is concerned primarily with his personal experiences and their expression. The descriptive philosophers, on the other hand, focuses on consciousness in a more detached way.

While a descriptive phenomenologist takes a neutral standpoint, an existentialist is primarily interested in his own experiences. As for example, when a patient tells a doctor about his ailments, his expression is 'confessional' i.e. how he *feels*. But when someone also tells a doctor how the patient behaves or feels, his expression is no longer 'confessional' rather it becomes descriptive. While existentialists accept the former approach, descriptive phenomenologists adopt the latter standpoint.

Both existentialists and the descriptive phenomenologists, nevertheless, are interested in consciousness. Once one grants that consciousness is not neutral (i.e. it is meaning bestowing) - as existentialists do, a confessional philosophy necessarily follows. For existentialists consciousness is meaningful in the context of individual existence. In Husserl's philosophy, however, it is only through the radical transcendental reductive method which puts existence into brackets, that consciousness shows itself in a purified form. The suspension of this method by the existentialists necessarily leads to existentialism. Existentialists, moreover, have developed the peculiar methodology which more than their common subject-matter unite them into a recognisable 'school' of philosophy. The methodology of existentialism consists in a perfectly deliberate and intentional use of *the concrete* as a way of approaching the abstract, the *particular* as a way of approaching the general.[23] It is perhaps this characteristic which has brought existentialists philosophy so near to literature and often so far from descriptive philosophy.

Compared to this, Husserl's kind of phenomenology shows itself as descriptive. He describes the immediate data of consciousness. However, it must be said that Husserl does not restrict to description throughout his philosophical career. Only the intermediate stage of his philosophy is descriptive. In the very early writings he was concerned with logical and mathematical problems. In the later works he was occcupied with the *construction* of the world or of worlds.

But throughout, Husserl's aim is to *clarify*. "Here arises – the great task of clarifying all our concepts whether they are our creations or are derived from the tradition . . . ."[24] Further he says, "Problems, like those concerning the meaning and object of knowledge, cannot be solved by subjecting them to some supposedly pure thinking . . . (but) by illuminating . . . through the laborious efforts of clarification and through clear apprehensions . . . .".[25] Philosophy of description is an activity of clarification. Clarification, however, is possible, for Husserl, only when philosophy does not presuppose anything. "In contrast to the presupposition – laden thinking"[26] Husserl advocated presuppositionless philosophy. The call to philosophize without presuppositions, of course, is nothing new. The empiricists reliance on observation as the utlimate source of knowledge was supposed to be equivalent to a presuppositionless philosophy. But there are certain presuppositions which are too fundamental to be dispensed with. When we speak of any claim to knowledge that we may have, we accept, as Michael Polanyi says, "a certain set of presuppositions and use them as our interpretative framework . . . ".[27] In this way no philosophy is totally presuppositionless, not even phenomenology. "In fact, the principle of presuppositionlessness has been called the greatest presupposition"[28] by Farber.

In twentieth century philosophy, the choice between description in the linguistic manner or the phenomenological manner is perhaps one of the crucial choices. The choice of description is presumably discretionary and the preference for one over another is no more a matter of science than of logic. The choice between one description over the other is more or less a matter of convenience rather than yes or no business which mere observation can settle. In addition to being accurate and relevant a good description may not be complete, it should be consistent, consistency being defined by implicit reference to the presumptive interest of qualified interlocutor. A good deal of discussion in contemporary philosophy is taken up with showing the sameness of their aims and methods or marking the differences between them. Findlay is usually quoted for his famous declaration that "Husserl's programme is, in fact, not very different from that of modern British and U.S. analytical philosophy."[29] It is not without significance that Husserl calls himself a "true positivist" and that Wittgenstein sponsors a "phenomenological language" or that Austin defines his philosophy as a "linguistic phenomenology". But while for Wittgenstein and Austin phenomena are linguistic and present themselves in a linguistic mode (i.e. we *identify* them through the use of language), Husserl's phenomena (i.e. essences) are neither linguistic nor mental. Rather they are what make both our language and our world meaningful. A phenomenologist attends to what he directly 'sees' in pure intuition. The analysts' investigations are carried on through the language. In each case the elucidatory process is emphasized strongly. But the analytical thinker speaks for the most part in terms of an objectivity simpliciter and the phenomenologist in terms of an objectivity which is *made possible* by subjectivity. Yet both of them are interested in a programme of clarification and in 'meaning'. But where lies the 'meaning' for them makes all the difference. The discussion of this question became the focus for a major debate in this century. In Husserl's philosophy meaning occupies a special status. To the phenomenologist meaning stems from the activity of the ego, whereas linguistic philosophy locates meaning in "the linguistic instrument". Yet it seems that Husserl's manifest meanings require language to express them and the analytical meanings of symbols and sentences are set up on a foundation of pre-verbal experiences. Language is tied up with what is, otherwise language would be set loose from contact with the world. We can't deny, of course, there is a gap between what one experiences and what one puts in language. That is why J.N. Mohanty strongly emphasizes that a descriptive philosopher is not a "speculative magician" but is a "tragic philosopher".[30] The tragic sense which accompanies a truly descriptive philosopher stems from the gulf which separates philosophic reflection and unreflective experience. The latter is never fully wrapped up in the former.

It is perhaps misleading to opt hastily for philosophical description on the pattern of either of the movements. For nothing less than the cooperative efforts of different types of philosophical investigations can be sufficient to lay the desired firm foundation for a descriptive philosophy which, in a sense, will always remain an ideal. The better strategy is to discuss critically the various descriptive programmes philosophers have adopted and to see to what extent they are actually descriptive. We confine ourselves to an examination of Wittgenstein and Husserl, for with respect to the issues under discussion they are undoubtedly thinkers of 'axial' importance.

References

1. Paul Grimley Kuntz quotes Josiah Royce, "Order in Language, Phenomena, and Reality : Notes On Linguistic Analysis, Phenomenology, And Metaphysics", *Monist,* Vol. 49, 1965, p. 132.

2. J.N. Mohanty, "Philosophical Description", *Philosophical Papers, First Series,* ed. by Kalidas Bhattacharyya, p 5

3. D.J.O. Connor, "Locke", *A Critical History of Western Philosophy,* ed. by D.J.O, Connor, p. 205.

4. Locke, *An Essay Concerning Human Understanding,* Abridged & Edited by A.D. Woosley, Book III, ii 2. p. 259.

5. *Cf.* J.N. Mohanty, "Philosophical Description", *Op. cit.* pp. 6-7.

6. *Cf.* W.G. Runciman, "Describing", *Mind,* Vol. LXXXI, July 1972.

7. *Cf.* Margaret Chatterjee, "Language as Phenomenon", *Philosophy and Phenomenological Research,* 1969, Vol. 30, p. 116.

8. *Cf.* B. Russell, *Human Knowledge : Its Scope and Limits,* pp. 516-52.

9. *Cf.* J.N. Mohanty, "The Given", read before the Delhi Philosophical Colloquium, reprinted in *Phenomenology and Ontology* by J.N. Mohanty, pp. 12-21.

10. D.A. McDougall, "'Descriptive' and 'Revisionary Metaphysics'", *Philosophy and Phenomenological Research,* Vol. 34, 1973, p. 214.

11. A.J. Ayer, *The Concept of a Person,* p. 28.

12. Nicholas Rescher, "Translation as a Tool of Philosophical Analysis", *Journal of Philosophy,* Vol. 53, 1956, p. 221.

13. L. Wittgenstein, *Philosophical Investigations,* para 220.

14. Ryle "Theory of Meaning", *British Philosophy in the Mid-Century,* ed. by C.A. Mace, p. 254.

15. *Cf.* Margaret Chatterjee, *op. cit.* p. 116.

16. *Cf.* G. Ryle, "Ordinary Language", *Ordinary Language* ed. by V.C. Chappell.

17. *Cf.* A. Flew, "Philosophy And Language", *Essays in Conceptual Analysis,* ed. by A. Flew. p. 7.

18. *Cf.* L. Wittgenstein, *Philosophical Investigations,* para 49.

19. E. Husserl, *Ideas I,* p. 214.

20. M. Heidegger, *Being and Time* (Eng. tr. of *Sein und Zeit*) by John Macquarrie, p. 59.

21. H. Heidegger, *Ibid.,* p. 61.

22. *Cf.* Margaret Chatterjee, *The Existentialist Outlook,* p. 3.

23. *Cf.* Mary Warnock, *Existentialism,* p. 133.

24. E. Husserl quoted by R. Schmitt, "Phenomenology and Analysis", *Philosophy and Phenomenological Research,* Vol. 23, 1962-63, p. 107.

25. *Ibid.,* p. 110.

26. Husserl quoted by Felix Kaufmann, *"Logical Empiricism"*, *Philosophical Essays in Memory of Edmund Husserl* ed. by Marvin Farber, p. 138.

27. M. Polanyi, *Personal Knowledge: Towards a Post-Critical Philosophy,* p. 60.

28. M. Farber, "The Idea of a Presuppositionless Philosophy", *Philosophical Eassys in Memory of Edmund Husserl* ed. by Marvin Farber, p. 44.

29. J.N. Findlay, "Phenomenology", *Encyclopedia Brittannica,* Vol. 17, 1963, p. 701.

30. J.N. Mohanty, "Philosophical Description", *Research in Phenomenology,* Vol. 14, p. 49.

2

Description in Wittgenstein's *Tractatus*

THE opening statement of the *Tractatus* "The world is all that is the case" reveals the central theme of the treatise. Wittgenstein's chief aim here is to describe the world. In spite of certain passages towards the end, the *Tractatus* is plainly a metaphysical work as Malcolm has noted.[1] Certain passages towards the end of the *Tractatus* show that language occupies a central place but Wittgenstein immediately adds, "He must transcend these propositions, and then he will see the world allright".[2] Even in the *Notebooks* Wittgenstein's interest was in "what is the case". He says "The great problem round which everything that I write turns is : Is there an order in the world *a priori*, and if so what does it consist in?"[3] This also states the chief problem of the *Tractatus*. He is concerned to describe the general structure of the world.

Wittgenstein, however, was never interested in providing knowledge about the factual world. He was only interested in elucidation of propositions con-cerning reality, as he says, "My propositions serve as elucidations."[4] Philosophical statements, he thought, are neither true nor false. They don't state or mis-state facts. Philosophical statements have a peculiar character. The problem of description in the *Tractatus* arises in the context of what this character is. Description here deals with *showing* the general structure of world than to *saying* anything about it. Philosophizing can, indeed, open our eyes to this structure, but it cannot issue significant statements about it. The "ladder has to be thrown" away later on.

The Philosoper's job is not to provide theories regarding the world. Wittgenstein says "Philosophy is not a body of doctrine but an activity"[5] of clarification. Its task is to expose the meaninglessness of propositions about the "limits" of the world which was the primary aim of traditional philosophers. Philosophical activities can be skilful or unskilful, successful or unsuccessful. It is in pursuing the activity itself that we see what philosophy is like. Like learning music or tennis, learning philosophy does not result in our being able to tell what we have learnt, though, as in music or tennis, we can show what we have learnt. Similarly philosophical clarity is achieved in the acts of appreciating arguments rather than in propounding theories. The philosopher or logician is debarred from stating things significantly or non-significantly. Philosophizing is the activity of exploring the internal logic of what is said.

The natural sciences deal with the description of the general structures of the world. But Wittgenstein differentiates philosophy from the sciences because scientific statements are different from philosophical statements. The former are essentially informative hence have truth value. For Russell, however, unlike for Wittgenstein, philosophical statements are scientific statements, and he did think that philosophers should aim at being as scientific as possible, as shown, for example, in the sub-title of his early work *Our Knowledge of the External World.* But for Wittgenstein, "Philosophy is not one of the natural sciences. (The word 'philosophy' must mean something whose place is above or below the natural sciences, not beside them)".[6] The object of philosophy is the logical clarification of thought. The result of philosophy is not a number of "philosophical propositions" but the clarification of propositions.

Wittgenstein's aim is to clarify and elucidate the logical structure of the world through clarifying language. Philosophers in the English speaking world are mainly responsible for having labelled Wittgenstein's philosophy as essentially linguistic. Max Black, for example, in *A Companion to Wittgenstein's Tractatus* states that the *Tractatus* is chiefly a linguistic treatise and all linguistic philosophers have been influenced by him in this respect. They think Wittgenstein's *Tractatus* actually brought about the 'linguistic turn' in philosophy. But this is not strictly correct, for language is treated therein only as a means and not as an end in itself. Language in the *Tractatus* is the medium for reaching reality. The world is pictured in language and it is treated as a mirror, 'the great mirror' which reflects reality. Language has only one function i.e. that of depicting the world. Description, consequently, here becomes depiction.

But why should only language be regarded as the gateway to reality? This comes about because Wittgenstein centres his discussion on modes of speaking. Analysis of modes of speaking can reveal what can be said and what can't be. Language is treated as a sieve which helps in sifting what can be said and what cannot be said. In Aristotelian philosophy there is a mode of rationality which helps in differentiating between true and false. Similarly in Kant there are modes of intuition and concepts which condition what can be known and what cannot be known. In the *Critique of Pure Reason* Kant's main question is, what must be the conditions which make synthetic a prior knowledge possible? On the other hand Wittgenstein, in an effort to provide the formal structure of reality through the structure of language, is providing a 'critique of language'. His main question in the *Tractatus* is, what conditions obtain so that language can be used in its assertive function to state true propositions about the world? This is neither an epistemological question nor linguistic one. It is, on the other hand, a metaphysical one.

Since Wittgenstein assumed that the function of language is to depict reality, an important question arises in this context. What is the nature of the language which fulfils this purpose? Is colloquial language fit for this job? In spite of contradictory views regarding the status of ordinary language in the *Tractatus,* Wittgenstein's opinion is that it is only a specially constructed language which can depict the structure of reality. He admits that ordinary language is logically complete in order, but it cannot serve philosophical purposes. All errors in philosophy arise because of the errors due to ordinary language. Philosophical problems arise through a confusion of the "apparent logical form" of propositions with their "real form". This corresponds to Russell's distinction between 'grammatical form' and 'logical form'. Wittgenstein acknowledges Russell's influence: "It was Russell who performed the service of showing that the apparent logical form of a proposition need not be its real one."[7] Ordinary language confuses sign with symbol. A sign is the perceptible structure of word while a symbol is sign as well as meaning. A symbol is more than a sign but nevertheless includes a sign. Sameness of sign is no guarantee of sameness of symbol. The same sign can be used in different symbols. But in ordinary language very frequently the use of the same sign means the use of the same symbol also. Making a distinction between sign and symbol, one can catalogue at least some of the confusions in the occurrence of 'is' as a copula, as sign of identity and also as a verb of existence. Far from having same meaning in these three cases, they are in fact three totally different symbols.[8] The logical form of ordinary language is not perspicuous because different modes of signification are expressed by physically similar signs. Wittgenstein suggests we can avoid these errors by reforming our language in such a way that signs themselves will make us aware of forms. In appropriate and artificial symbolism differences of forms in symbols is embodied in difference of form in signs. Therefore, philosophers must employ a symbolism which excludes philosophical problems. Wittgenstein felt the need of a new faultless language. To him job of the philosopher is to construct an ideography which would manifestly obey the rules of logical syntax.

Ideal language was not a discovery, something uncovered beneath the confusing wrappings of ordinary language; it was something totally new, invented, constructed. It is made of precise symbols along with explicit rules of their combinations. A constructed language is sign language which is governed by 'logical grammar' and 'logical syntax' in place of ordinary grammar. The language of *Principia Mathematica* is the model for the constructed language of the *Tractatus*. Wittgenstein thought this language had the capacity to reveal the structure of reality. The basic structure of reality, for Wittgenstein, cannot be known empirically. He can have access to this only through the ideal language of atomic propositions which alone represents or pictures the structure of the world. The new language may be "perspicuous language", for purpose of this language is to show perspicuously what is hidden.[9] Or the new language may be called a "ladder language" which has to be thrown away after solving philosophical problems.[10] In any case it is clear that ordinary language will not do and that there is a need for a logically perfect language which is governed by logical syntax and obeys 'logical grammar'. The difference between ideal language and ordinary language in this respect is that while in the latter case it is hard to discern logical syntax in the former case it is hard not to see it.

The new language is truth-functional in nature. The language consists of elementary propositions and their combinations. Elementary propositions with the help of logically binary operations give rise to complex propositions. The elementary propositions are combined through these binary operations which function as connectives. They connect one elementary proposition with another. Given all possible elementary propositions one could construct any number of propositions from them by using only truth-functional operatives. The logical connectives are thus indispensable syntactical devices. This process claims to cover the entire field of language for language is the totality of elementary and complex propositions.

Moreover, the truth or falsity of complex proposition depends on the truth or falsity of their constituents i.e. on elementary propositions. A complex "proposition is an expression of agreement and disagreement with truth-possibilities of elementary propositions."[11] Further Wittgenstein says "Truth-possibilities of elementary propositions are the conditions of the truth and falsity of propositions".[12]

As in the case of the structure of language, the structure of the world is also truth-functional. The world consists of both simple and complex facts. Molecular facts are truth functions of atomic facts. Even if the world is infinitely complex in the sense that every complex fact consists of infinitely many state of affairs, it is resolved into atomic facts. Entire reality is a combination of atomic facts. Atomic facts are units out of which system of reality is built. Atomic facts are the ultimate bricks of the world in the sense that world is constructed out of them. In *Tractatus* both language and reality are atomic in structure. Clearly this is to follow a model; the model drawn from Chemistry.

How is the elementary proposition obtained? Wittgenstein, like Russell, thinks this comes about by a process of logical analysis which yields up basic propositions. "It is obvious that the analysis of propositions must bring us to elementary propositions which consist of names in immediate combination"[13] It is a logical matter that complexes should be analyzed into simples and it is also a matter of logic that the process of analysis should come to an end, should have a terminus somewhere. 'Analysis', for Russell and Wittgenstein, meant resolving complex into ultimate elements incapable of further resolutions. Search for ultimate logical indefinables runs like a connecting thread through *Notes on Logic, Notebooks* and the *Tractatus* in Wittgenstein's philosophy. He also applies the process of logical analysis to reality. Analysis of complex reality gives atomic facts, *tatsache,* or *Sachverhalt* (states of affairs). Wittgenstein like Descartes is trapped into natural temptation to seek absolute simple - a temptation which had led generations of philosophers astray. System of language and of reality in the *Tractatus* is based on this assumption. This takes us back to rationalists programme, which is certainly not descriptive in character.

Moreover, the characteristics of simplicity and complexity have meaning in a context and are not fixed in nature of thing. No object or fact by nature is simple or complex. Wittgenstein wrongly assumed that there is such a thing as simple fact or situation in world. Main trouble with Wittgenstein's descriptive programme in the *Tractatus* is his assumption that there is one and only one final analysis of anything including propositions. For since it is possible to specify constituents of a thing in such radically different ways, it is most unlikely that all these analysis when pushed ahead will in every field have same final result. In spite of the fact that purpose of Wittgenstein's analysis is to clarify yet it ignores the possibility of diversities of analysis.

Wittgenstein based his descriptive programme on truth-functional theory of language. Since both structure of language and structure of world is truth-functional, depiction of later into former is possible. But every proposition does not depict reality. Only elementary proposition can do it. "First and foremost the elementary propositional form must portray; all portrayal takes place through it".[14] Simplest proposition depicts simplest part of reality. However, it is form of world which is being depicted and not content. Pictorial form is basis of depiction. Form of reality is mirrored in form of language. The idea that language is a model of reality came to Wittgenstein when he was serving in the Austrian Army in the First World War. He saw a newspaper that described occurrence and location of an automobile accident by means of a diagram or map. It occurred to Wittgenstein that this map was a proposition and that therein revealed essential nature of propositions, namely, they model reality.[15]

However, it is state of affairs, facts and not objects which are being pictured and described: "A proposition is a description of a state of affairs".[16] The smallest unit of reality is atomic fact and world is totality of these facts. Facts have privileged status in the *Tractatus.* But they are constituted of objects which are described but not referred to. "Situations can be described but not *given* names".[17] Two types of relations are recognised in the *Tractatus,* naming and describing. They are different from each other. As Wittgenstein says later in the *Philosophical Investigations,* "naming and describing do not stand on the same level; naming is a preparation for description".[18] The *Tractatus* is concerned mainly with describing.

Now the discussion of description in the *Tractatus* is grafted on to a method modelled on mathematics. But the *Principia Mathematica* model actually gives *no* description at all because it is based on the model of a logical calculus which is purely deductive. Both Russell and Wittgenstein used the method of analysis to solve philosophical problems. The aim of analysis is to reduce complex language as well as reality to their simpler constituents. In order to carry this out they use mathematically oriented truth-functional language to build systems which are certainly not compatible with the descriptive programme. The whole programme of philosophy as description is incompatible with constructing ideal language. The former is non-mathematical and contented with what is there before us, instead of inventing something new. Language is not a mirror of reality, nor a clue to certain basic constituents. It is a natural *activity* undertaken by ordinary people with concrete aims in view. Ordinary speech is recalcitrant to any fixed logical framework.[19] Once we try to deal with real state of affairs, we find that symbolic logic would exclude the possibility of fresh situations arising and thus debar us from using language for new cases. Language would be so to say a closed system with strict boundaries. Even the slightest violation of boundaries is not permitted in symbolic language. But actually language is ever flowing and resists any fixed pattern of mathematical calculation. Language is an activity. It is often called into service in new situations. Moreover, truth-functional theory cannot be applied to all complex propositions.

The picture theory in Wittgenstein's philosophy is dependent on truth function theory. The latter is enlisted in depicting the world. Anscombe goes as far as to say that Wittgenstein's truth-functional theory is not only related to the picture theory but rather that both of them are one and the same.[20] If truth functional theory collapses so does the picture theory. Wittgenstein's picture theory also suffers from all traditional objections put against the theory of correspondence. One of these is that we must know reality intuitively in order to be able to say that language pictures reality. Behind the argument in the *Tractatus* lies the important question what the world would look like when not mirrored in language. Wittgenstein admits at the end of the *Tractatus* that this he cannot tell. "Throughout his life, Wittgenstein was like a man obsessed with the question of what he looks like when he is *not* looking in a mirror. *Ex hypothesi;* he can never know. In the *Tractatus,* he tells us in detail, and *also* tells us summarily and at the end, that he *cannot tell*".[21] In fact, Wittgenstein himself later realised the mistakes of the picture theory and in *Philosophical Investigations,* he confessed, "A *picture* held us captive"[22] in the *Tractatus.*

A prejudice arises from some pervasive features of our thought or language that the structure of reality is revealed through the structure of language. On what grounds do we say that situation and proposition have the same logical form? It seems that this is not more than an assumption, and a dogmatic and misleading assumption at that. The picture theory wrongly assumes that there is a natural appropriateness of structural likeness between language and reality. But this is nothing but a theorist's fantasy. In the words of Warnock, it is a case of seeming to see in heavens a pattern that is really marked out on the lens of the telescope.[23] This also justifies the observation of Ernest Gellner that "The alleged cognisable atoms of the world, postulated to correspond to the ultimate atoms of language, were not merely hard to locate and identify and describe plausibly, they also had a metaphysical air. It is difficult to resist the impression . . . that they are simply a kind or reduplication of a surmised linguistic atom, invented as its shadow".[24] Moreover, Wittgenstein insists that in philosophy we should not accept any ineffable truth and yet the theory of description in the *Tractatus* is based on an alleged important and ineffable truth, namely that the pre-lingual world was such as would be reflected in a perfect language.

The theme of the *Tractatus* appears to be that reality is known through language only. There is nothing outside it. But one passage in the *Tractatus* goes against this assumption. "A proposition, therefore, does not actually contain its sense, but does contain the possibility of expressing it . . .. A proposition contains the form, but not the content, of its sense".[25]

Language gets its sense from reality which is outside language. Reality exists by itself. It has objectivity. Though Wittgenstein kept philosophy apart from the sciences, he yet stressed objectivity in philosophy, which is, after all, a main characteristic of the sciences. Moreover, a proposition has a sense only when it depicts a fact. This appears to be the *Tractatus* theme. In this situation how will negative propositions acquire sense? It seems that a false proposition has sense only when it depicts a negative fact and this is a surprisingly Meinongian position to adopt.[26] One wonders how the *Tractatus* which is generally anti-Meinongian, can adopt this position.

Moreover, in spite of the fact that the *Tractatus* is non-speculative, Wittgenstein is not hostile to metaphysics in this work. He says, "Don't think I despise metaphysics or ridicule it. On the contrary, I regard the great metaphysical writings of the past as among the noblest productions of the human mind".[27] There is "fragment of metaphysics in his philosophy, in his picture theory of language".[28] But Wittgenstein's metaphysical system is that of 'logical atomism' and this differentiates him from the speculative metaphysicians. The phrase 'logical atomism' was coined by Russell[29] with the prospect in view that the philosopher can get down in theory if not in practice, to ultimate simples, out of which the world is built and that those simples have a kind of reality not belonging to anything else. Wittgenstein's system makes the same assumption.

Wittgenstein had a fixed ontology to which he was committed right from the beginning. For him the world is constituted of facts, simple and complex. Wittgenstein, however, breaks away sharply from the traditional trend. Against the background of earlier metaphysics, the outstanding innovation of Wittgenstein's ontology is his characterization of the universe as an aggregate of facts and not of things. In fact, the *Tractatus* opens with the remark "The word is totality of facts, *not* of things".[30] This sets him apart from Aristotle, Descartes, Spinoza, indeed from any of classical philosophers. When they search for truths of the highest generality about the universe, they usually conceive themselves to be investigating some nameable entity. But for Wittgenstein the universe cannot be *referred* to by name. It can only be described. State of affairs are *experienced* and hence described instead of being simply referred to. In one sense, no doubt, Wittgenstein in the *Tractatus* is committed to a general over-arching system of metaphysics. Nothing could be more metaphysical than such statements that only objects "make up the substance of the world." They are simple and indestructible. Behind the metaphysics of 'logical atomism' and the truth-functional theory was an assumption that the constituents and especially the ultimate constituents of the world are present in the very nature of things. In other words, to interpret the world as the totality of facts is also to adopt a specific attitude towards reality. There are equally valid alternative ways of "dividing up" the world; one of them might be more convenient or illuminating for some purposes, while others serve better for different purposes. Wisdom suggests that "an account of the world in terms of things, an account of the world in terms of facts and an account of the world in terms of events are just accounts of one world in three languages".[31] Wittgenstein wrongly thought that there is only one right answer to the question what the ultimate constituents of the world are.

Moreover, Wittgenstein maintains not only that the world consists merely of facts but that each fact is uniquely described. He thus failed to see that facts are capable of multiple descriptions. His contention that some things are absolutely simple seems here to amount to maintaining that language in general is a fixed system whose resources for description are necessarily limited to a fixed set of names. Actually a fact can be described in many ways.

Wittgenstein thought there is just *one* complete and perfect description of the world. He thus rules out the possiblity of multiple descriptions of the world. Now Wittgenstein differentiated philosophical description from scientific description precisely because the latter is incapable of providing one true description of the world. Scientific description changes with new discoveries. Wittgenstein says, "In scientific description, there is no such thing as 'complete' description and every measurement leaves room for further accuracy of specification".[32] No system of scientific laws describes the world once for all. The world can be described more accurately by one system of mechanics than by another. New discoveries replace old ones. Philosophical description, on the other hand, Wittgenstein thinks, is one and changeless. Combinations of elementary propositions provide all encompassing description of the world. For Wittgenstein "If all true elementary propositions are given, the result is complete description of the world".[33] But philosophical description, no less than scientific description is always changing. It is something dynamic, shifting and not static. Moreover, we cannot always fix the limits of situations and their composition in advance, either logically or mathematically. This depends on the nature of concrete situations. Simple correspondence between language and fact is ruled out for the simple reason that language enters into the very constitution of facts and the facts cannot be cut off from actual situation and human life. In maintaining that the world has a given structure the *Tractatus*, it seems to us, hangs between the traditional philosophical approach and the descriptive programme. It is betwixt and between. This is, of course, one of the chief reasons why Wittgenstein himself changes his standpoint in his later work.

References

1. *Cf.* N. Malcolm, Book Review of *English Philosophy since 1900;* (G.J. Warnock), *Philosophical Review,* Vol. 68, 1959, p. 257.
2. L. Wittgenstein, *Tractatus Logico-Philosophicus,* Eng. tr. by D.F. Pears and B.F. McGuinness, Paperback Edition 1974, 6.54 (2).
3. L. Wittgenstein, *Notebooks,* 1914-16, entry 2.6.15, p. 53e.
4. L. Wittgenstein, *Tractatus,* 6.54.
5. *Ibid.,* 4.112.
6. *Ibid.,* p. 111.
7. *Ibid.,* 4.0031.
8. *Cf.* J. Griffin, *Wittgenstein's Logical Atomism,* Griffin shows the difference among different uses of a sign by putting them in different types of brackets which he calls the "bracket language", pp. 134-35.
9. *Cf.* W. Sellers, "Naming & Saying", *Essays on Wittgenstein's Tractatus,* ed. by I.M. Copi. etc. p. 251.
10. Richard J. Bernstein, "Wittgenstein's Three Language", *Essays on Wittgenstein's Tractatus,* ed. by I.M. Copi. etc. pp. 236-37.
11. L. Wittgenstein, *Tractatus,* 4.4.
12. *Ibid.,* 4.41.
13. *Ibid.,* 4.221.
14. L. Wittgenstein, *Notebooks,* entry on 31.10.14, p. 226.
15. *Cf.* N. Malcolm, *Ludwig Wittgenstein : A Memoir,* p. 68.
16. L. Wittgenstein, *Tractatus,* 4.023.
17. *Ibid.,* 3.144.
18. L. Wittgenstein, *Philosophical Investigations,* para 49.
19. *Cf.* G. Ryle, "Ordinary Language", *op. cit.*
20. G.E.M. Anscombe, *An Introduction to Wittgenstein's Tractatus,* p. 81.
21. E. Gellner, *Words and Things,* p. 131.

22. L. Wittgenstein, *Philosophical Investigations,* para 115.

23. *Cf.* G.J. Warnock, *English Philosophy Since 1900,* p. 87.

24. E. Gellner *op. cit,* p. 74.

25. L. Wittgenstein, *Tractatus,* 3.13.

26. *Cf.* James Bogen, *Wittgenstein's Philosophy of Language,* pp. 26, 113-14, pp. 118-19.

27. N. O'C Drury quotes Wittgenstein, "A Symposium on Wittgenstein", *Ludwig Wittgenstein : Man and His Philosophy,* ed. by K.T. Fann, p. 68 (also *Cf.* p. 120).

28. C.A. Van Peursen, *Ludwig Wittgenstein,* p. 72.

29. *Cf.* B. Russell, "The Philosophy of Logical Atomism", reprinted in *Logic and Knowledge,* ed. by Bobert C. Marsh, pp. 175-281.

30. L. Wittgenstein, *Tractatus,* 1.1.

31. John Wisdom, "Logical Constructions" Part II, *Mind,* 1931, Vol. 40, p. 460.

32. Max Black, *A Companion to Wittgenstein's Tractatus* p. 353.

33. L. Wittgenstein, *Tractatus* 4.26.

3

Description in Wittgenstein's Later Works

In his later works Wittgenstein's aim and method is, in his own words, "*purely* descriptive". The descriptive method of philosophy is contrasted with the explanatory method of the natural sciences. If we use the explanatory method in philosophy we *cause* problems rather than solve them. Explanation generates false theories and contradictory philosophical systems. Wittgenstein says his aim is "not to advance any kind of theory. There must not be anything hypothetical in our considerations. We must do away with all *explanation,* and description alone must take its place".[1]

This is the standpoint Wittgenstein reached on the basis of two considerations, namely, to explain natural phenomena is the unique function of science and that philosophy is most emphatically not science. From this he concludes that the method of science can never be the method for philosophy. Scientific method "reduces" natural phenomena to the smallest possible number of primitive natural laws. Philosophers constantly see the method of science before their eyes and are irresistibly tempted to ask and answer question in the way that science does. But this leads philosophy into complete darkness. Science solves puzzlements and mental discomfort when we fail to understand certain facts. But when systems or notations of our language do not satisfy us, philosophy must step in. Causal explanation presupposes a certain understanding of linguistic phenomena, a certain use of language and this Wittgenstein thought is precisely what a philosopher who is confused about language, lacks.

Philosophers are not interested in empirical scientific questions to which explanations in the form of hypotheses about causes are relevant. Causes are "hidden" and are not directly observable. The scientist devises hypotheses about what may reveal hidden causes. But in philosophy nothing is "hidden" in the sense that what is "hidden" falls outside the purview of philosophy. Things which philosophers are looking for 'already lie open to view' and have escaped their attention because they are too evident to be seriously considered.

The function of philosophy is to "assemble reminders" of the obvious. It is of this that the actual *pattern* of uses is to be made clear. Everything in the pattern is, however, perfectly familiar to us already. "Philosophy simply puts everything before us, and neither explains nor deduces anything. Since everything lies open to view there is nothing to explain. For what is hidden . . . is of no interest to us."[2] Expecting something extra-ordinary philosophers go in pursuit of chimeras. Looking for something with a halo, they miss what is humble; dazed by thought of an ideal, they failed to see what is actual.

What then does a philosopher describe? While in the *Tractatus* Wittgenstein thought the philosophers described reality, in his later works he thinks the proper task of philosophers is to describe the various uses of language, for philosophical problems arise through mystifying uses of language. What makes it possible to say something is the problem that continues to lie at the centre of all his writings till the very end. In his earlier philosophy a proposition *(Satz)* says something because it is a picture or model of reality. In his later account, a sentence represents a 'move in a language-game'; it is a 'tool' used to accomplish a particular purpose. Instead of logic of 'truth-conditions' he relies on a logic of 'use-conditions'. The 'use-conditions' when considered specifically with respect to the cognitive uses of language, have to do with the grounds or evidences to which one can appeal to justify the acceptance of a particular proposition.

Errors in the uses of language are sources of philosophical puzzles. "Philosophy is a battle against the bewitchment of our intelligence by means of language".[3] But this bewitchment is not without a remedy. We can battle against it by careful description of how people use words and sentences in various ways. "The problems are solved, not by giving new information, but by arranging what we have always known".[4] The country is well known to us, so we need only to be *reminded* of our whereabouts. Moreover, in order to correct errors of language Wittgenstein does not construct new language, he does not try to improve on, or to tamper with language, but only describes its working. For confusions arise not when language is doing its work but when "language *goes on holiday*". "The confusions which occupy us arise when language is like an engine idling, not when it is doing work".[5] It is when philosophers consider words and sentences in abstraction from their linguistic and non-linguistic contexts that they seem to conceal a mystry and invite a myth. So philosophers are to 'assemble reminders' about their use, not at random, nor yet systematically, but on such occasion with some particular purpose in view, dispelling some particular confusions and making clear the ways in which words actually function. For every philosophical problem it is of basic importance to acquire a wide-ranging familiarity with uses, to assemble many details about uses. Such indeed, he thinks, is what philosophizing is about.

Wittgenstein, of course, says that 'we assemble reminders' of the language for a particular purpose, but a purpose is not just given. It has to be hunted out, it has to be argued and presented. The solutions of philosophical problems are not found only in 'assembling reminders', for besides this, the philosopher must select and arrange them in such a way that he comes to get some picture of the landscape.[6] The very purpose of philosophical investigation compels a man to travel over a wide region of uses, 'criss-cross' in every direction. Some uses are examined again and again, each time from a different direction and from a different point of view. These various sketches do not of themselves fall together to form a picture. They are to be *arranged* in such a way that if one looks at them one can get a picture of the landscape and so to some extent get to know one's way about. The importance of *finding* and *inventing* intermediate cases cannot be ruled out. Rather they seem to be indispensable. Only by finding, inventing and arranging views does the philosopher get to know his way "out of the fly-bottle". The language so to speak becomes "surveyable", not by passive watching of what "already lies open to view" but by something further. It is not that the cases always just come before us for often cases can be invented and arranged.

The process of 'assembling reminders' was for Wittgenstein a non-argumentative activity – a matter of simple description. Yet paradoxically, he puts his views forward through arguments. These are not in the form of technical procedures or the symbolism used in specialized fields. His argumentation is rather the kind people adopt when they want to convince anyone of almost any sort of disputable conclusion, say, to show that the methods of some new branch of psychology have not made good their claim to be scientific, or that, given his record, John Doe is not the man to be entrusted with responsibilities. Such cases are instances of arguments *par* excellence and Wittgenstein's later philosophy certainly uses such arguments.[7] These arguments are not speculative or deductive, they are natural. But reasoning is there nonetheless.

Wittgenstein argued that language has different uses and serves different purposes but philosophers have wrongly understood the function of language. To grant that language has a multiple character sheds a new light on philosophical problems. Wittgenstein's aim was to "bring words back from their metaphysical to their everyday use", destroy the "houses of cards" and clear up the "ground of language on which they stand." The purpose of philosophy is "seeing connections", rearranging concepts, finding and inventing intermediate cases. The main purpose of describing the various uses of language is to expose the confusions which underline traditional philosophical problems. In the *Blue Book* as well as in the *Philosophical Investigations* Wittgenstein exposed the "myth of meaning." He finds that most philosophical problems arise because of a wrong theory of meaning. Philosophers are wrongly misled by attributing substantive meanings to words and language. They ask "What is beauty?", "What is time?" as if beauty or time are substances to which we can refer, as if in our usual forms of expression there were "something hidden that has to be brought to light". They thus look for 'universals' as the meanings of general words. The problem of meaning is thereby related to a "craving for generality". Along with this diagnosis Wittgenstein rejected the view which regards mental occurrences as the *source* of meaning or as something lying beneath or behind meaning. The image theory of meaning gave rise to many philosophical problems. Inner meanings for Wittgenstein are a "grammatical fiction" in the sense that they have no role in the learning and using our language. Wittgenstein does not deny that inner images exist or occur, but only denies that they are necessary to our ordinary use of language. Instead of looking for hidden essences purporting to be the meaning of words like 'knowledge', 'being', 'object', 'understanding', 'I', 'name', 'proposition' etc., we should "look how the words in question *are actually used in our language*". The meaning of word does not stem from private a *priori* expressions but from the entire corpus of social conventions. A sentence gets its meaning in the system of language. Instead of looking for meanings of words we should in fact ask for their uses. "Don't ask for the meaning ask for the use", is the recommendation. The understanding of a word means having been trained to use that word. Since 1930s Wittgenstein stressed that signs by themselves are dead and only use give them life.[8]

Words are like tools and are capable of various uses. "Think of the tools in a tool-box: there is a hammer, pliers, a saw, a screw-driver, a ruler, a glue-pot, glue, nails and screws. The functions of words are as diverse as the functions of these objects".[9] Wittgenstein's comparison of words to tools unmistakably emphasizes their instrumental nature. "Look at the sentence as an instrument, and at its sense as its employment".[10] Language is an instrument which is used variously. To invent a language could mean to invent an instrument for a particular purpose. We should, therefore, not look for just one function common to all types of word-uses. Language had just one function in the *Tractatus* i.e. to describe the essential structures of the world. Wittgenstein's interest was then primarily in structure. In the later works this was abandoned in the interest of a still greater commitment of description. One of the main advantages of the doctrine of polymorphism is that it rejects the reductive analysis which was practised in the *Tractatus*. Description of various uses of language frees philosophers from the temptation to seek a reduction of one kind of expression to another.

However, it is not only through wrong uses of language that mistakes in philosophy come about, but wrong grammer is no less responsible. For Russell grammar is often the villain. Like Russell, he refers us to logical grammar in place of ordinary grammar. He found that it is ordinary grammar which confuses philosophers. The uncovering of logical grammar can remove such confusions. Wittgenstein often says that philosophical investigations mean 'grammatical investigations'. Philosophical problems are due to 'grammatical confusions'. Problems in philosophy arise when words in our ordinary language have *prima facie* analogous grammars and we are inclined to try to interpret them analogously. To avoid grammatical errors Wittgenstein provides 'grammatical analysis' and 'grammatical notes'. It is important to note that grammatical analysis is for him descriptive rather than explanatory. "The scrutiny of the grammar of a word weakens the position of certain fixed standards of our expression which had prevented us from seeing facts with unbiased eyes. Our investigation tried to remove this bias, which forces us to think that the facts *must* conform to certain pictures embedded in our language".[11] Philosophy thus, for Wittgenstein, becomes fight against grammar. In the *Tractatus* he replaced ordinary grammar by logical grammar, and in his later works he replaced surface grammar (which generates problems) by depth grammar. It seems that the wrong use of words and the wrong use of grammar are co-eval terms. A philosopher has to protect himself from both of them.

The word 'grammar', however, has a vastly extended meaning for Wittgenstein, a meaning far wider than the ordinary one. Sometimes he speaks of grammatical form as 'a mode of representation'. Grammar, it seems, is the form in which we represent words: it is like a scheme which serves different purposes. We cannot speak of things without employing some form of grammar. For Wittgenstein grammar is what replaces mataphysics and epistemology and is prior to both of them. "Grammar is not accountable to any reality. It is grammatical rules that determine meaning (constitute it) and so they themselves are not answerable to any meaning and to that extent are arbitrary".[12] Grammar is autonomous; thought (and the language that conveys it) has its internal structures as articulated by the grammatical rules that belong to it. The choice of these rules or the grammar of thought is not to be determined by establishing some isomorphic relation to reality. Reality does not have independent structure to which our language considered as a *system of rules* conforms and to which it must stand in a relation of formal identity. Rather, thought (language is structured by human conventions) brings to reality its own structure. In order to describe reality one must use these pre-established 'forms of thought' (rules of grammar). It is through the use and application of these rules that one can deal with reality in a 'thoughtful' (linguistic) way. One cannot give a description of reality that does not already use some grammatical rule in giving such a description. Throughout his philosophical career Wittgenstein is obsessed by the question what is the connection between language and reality? In his earlier works he thinks that the meaning (sense) of linguistic expression is to be determined by correlation with some antecedently and independently existing structures of reality; whereas in his later works he believes the connection between language and reality is made by us, not by means of queer and instantaneous mental acts, but in our activity. Our activity is itself a connection. A sentence represents a 'move in a language-game'; it is a tool used to accomplish a particular purpose, though not necessarily or exclusively one of describing reality; its sense is governed by various grammatical rules.

Grammatical rules are implicit in language in the way the rules of a game are implicit in the game. "Grammar describes the use of words in the language. So it has somewhat the same relation to the language as the description of a game, the rules of a game, have to the game".[13] Wittgenstein's concept of a 'grammatical rule' like grammar itself has a very different meaning from its customary sense. The rules of grammar are *conventions*. They are neither true nor false. On the other hand, one may assert various *propositions* that purport to describe same segment of reality. Such propositions are either true or false. However, the formulation of these propositions rests upon and makes use of various grammatical conventions. Their sense (if not their actual truth or falsity) is based on the use of some grammatical rule (or rules). The justification of the grammatical rules does not rest on the propositions; it is the other way round the sense of the proposition rests on the grammatical system it employs and its truth or falsity upon what we find to be the case. Since there are any number of possible ways of describing reality by using one or another grammatical rule in giving such descriptions, there is no absolute or language-independent preferential status that attaches to one rule rather than another; there are no reasons in the nature of things to justify the adoption of one rule rather than another. We are obliged to use some method of representation, and this already commits us to the use of some language scheme. The adoption of one rather than another language system for accomplishing a description cannot be supported by appealing to reality. It is in this sense that the adoption of any language system is arbitrary. It would make no sense to say, for example, that the metric system, as contrasted with the British Imperial system, is the one according to which Nature 'really' works. Any system one adopts is a matter of convention. One cannot appeal to some description of reality by which one can justify or to give reasons for the adoption of some grammatical rule or system of grammatical rules, linguistic system or conceptual scheme.

These devices (languages or conceptual schemes) are to be judged by their effectiveness in accomplishing human purposes. The standards used in making judgements of effectiveness are on the whole pragmatic one. How effective, how successful and how convenient any linguistic system is, that is going to decide whether that scheme is accepted by men. In other words the rules of grammer formulate *criteria* for the meaning of a term. Criteria are adopted as a matter of convention; but their adoption calls for a decision.

The study of grammar is one of the important functions of philosophy. The failure to engage in this study accounts for the puzzlements, entanglements in pseudo problems, and confusions that pervade much of traditional philosophy. The task of genuine philosophy is to free us from these snares. In becoming clear about the grammar of our language we achieve philosophical enlightenment. The goal of philosophy is to achieve a perspicuous representation, to command a clear view of the use of our words and to produce understanding through coming to see connections. "The concept of perspicuous representation is of fundamental significance for us. It earmarks the form of the account we give, the way we look at things".[14] This is clearly a *'Weltanschauung'*. Thus, at least, though indirectly and despite its speaking "nonsense", philosophy can and does formulate an ontology.

The interesting thing in Wittgenstein's philosophy is that although problems in philosophy arise because of grammatical confusions yet these errors have to be avoided by grammar itself. Errors arise from 'surface grammar' and can be rectified through 'depth grammar'. Wittgenstein does not provide a definition of 'surface grammar' or 'depth grammar'. He provides only examples. Surface grammar is a source of illusions and mystifications, creating puzzles and seemingly insoluble problems for philosophy. On the surface, grammar is full of wrong similes which create false appearances and pictures which force themselves on us. It fascinates us with misleading analogies and tempts us to invent myths. Surface grammar is thus a source of delusion. Of surface grammar Wittgenstein says, "What immediately impresses itself upon us about the use of a word is the way it is used in the construction of the sentence, the part of its use – one might say – that can be taken in by the ear."[15] Surface grammar suggests that impressions provide pictures. But a whole nest of philosophical problems will be generated if we push this point.

Ordinary language which is governed by 'surface grammar' leads philosophers astray. Wrongly they assume that words have one fixed meaning and are used only in one way under the influence of surface grammar. "We remain unconscious of the prodigious diversity of all the everyday language-games because the clothing of our language makes everything alike",[16] says Wittgenstein. However, it is through the analysis of ordinary language, through probing into the depth of language that the infinite uses of words are made clear. The differences which are hidden by the uniform appearance of written and spoken words can be revealed by examining their correct grammar.

Wittgenstein believes that ordinary language is deceptive and bewitched. Though sentences in ordinary language are in perfect logical order just as they stand, yet they deceive philosophers. Wittgenstein cites the same example he uses in the *Tractatus* to illustrate the errors generated by ordinary language. There is a difference between 'is' in 'The rose is red', 'Two and two is four' and 'There is no God'.

The conclusion following from this is that it is impossible to follow ordinary language when doing philosophy. What then should we do? Should philosophers construct a new language which is free from the deficiencies of ordinary language? Wittgenstein, of course, does not go back in the direction of the *Tractatus* which he leaves behind. He rather analyses ordinary language itself. However, Wittgenstein thinks the need for the analysis of ordinary language arises not because of some intrinsic defect in ordinary language but because philosophers failed to see its *multiple character.* The analysis of ordinary language takes us to a deeper level, a level where we see many uses of languages and varieties of language games. The task of analysis is to help us become aware of the 'grammars', the rules of grammars as well as the contexts of daily livings in which the expressions and constructions of language find their use. We study these rules by attending to the different kinds of language-games we 'play'. What we examine is the similarities and differences among the roles and uses to which the different 'pieces' (the expressions) of language are put in playing our language games.

Depth grammar solves the problems created by apparent grammar. What is depth grammar and how can we reach it? The answer to this question, which is the chief aim of Wittgenstein's later philosophy, seems to go against the main thrust of the descriptive programme. Depth grammar probes innumerable, sometimes incomplete forms of language as these are to be discovered in actual language. When depth grammar is discussed, it appears to involve some very simple rules, though these are extremely difficult to apply in the various uses that we find in everyday language. The analysis of depth grammar is concerned with the discovery of what is actually given. We ignore the pattern present in a whole range of uses by fixing our gaze on one of them as one might ignore the pattern in a carpet by looking at it in wrong way. We do not need to look at a carpet with special instruments or to turn it over and examine it underneath which was roughly the proposal of the *Tractatus,* but need to change our attitude towards it and to free ourselves from the constrictions of a routine.

Ordinary language holds our mind rigidly in one position and this causes mental cramp. The task of depth grammar is to remove this mental cramp. The aim of depth grammar is to obtain philosophical clarity. Wittgenstein's ambitious goal is to achieve *complete clarity* which consists in the complete disappearance of philosophical problems. To analyse ordinary language is to uncover its 'depth grammar' and this means to locate use of words in a particular language-game. Depth grammar is certainly hidden in our use of words. Philosophers have to search for it. A veil has to be removed in order to see it. But is it not something 'hidden' which we can get only after analyzing ordinary language? On the one hand, Wittgenstein says we need depth-grammar in order to remove puzzles but, on the other hand, he says we do not have to "dig" to see how language functions. One wonders how Wittgenstein maintains both these views. The distinction between 'surface grammar' and 'depth grammar' certainly suggests the idea of concealment. His concept of 'depth grammar' does not lie open to view; it also has to be dug out. What lies before us is merely the 'surface grammar'.

Wittgenstein argues that a certain form of expression *obscures* a certain possibility, something as it were hidden which another way (other than the ordinary way) of speaking might make clearer. The same point comes out a little later in the *Blue Book* when Wittgenstein says that certain forms of expression hide "grammatical rules". The proposition "I cannot feel his pain" embodies certain grammatical rules which must be made obvious as a preliminary to discussion of other (and better) rules. Ordinarily speaking, a grammatical rule is not something which is 'hidden' by a particular form of expression – rather it is a rule which can be given a precise meaning and according to which sentences must conform if they are to be grammatically correct. On more than one occasion, however, Wittgenstein writes as if a grammatical rule is something which may often be concealed by an ordinary expression and this does not square with the view that "everything lies open to view . . . (and) what is hidden . . . is of no interest to us."[17] True, he does say that aspects of things that are most important for us are hidden because of their simplicity and familiarity, that is, to say, ignored because they are so evident. But this is not always his meaning when he speaks of something being 'hidden'. A 'grammatical rule' which is 'hidden' by an ordinary form of expression which may even on the surface suggests a different rule, can hardly be said to be familiar or obvious.

This seems to indicate that Wittgenstein's attitude to ordinary language is far from unambiguous. If ordinary language is perfectly logically in order, and even the vaguest sentence is "in order as it is" and all that is to be done is to study what lies clearly before us than why should it ever be necessary or advantageous for philosophers to device language games, 'clear and simple language-games' which serve as "objects of comparison" or "measuring rode" and which "throw light on the facts of our language"? Wittgenstein, of course, grants that ordinary language is not insufficient for our practical purposes, "but that it is slightly cumbrous and sometimes misleading." It is because of this that Wittgenstein felt it necessary to discover 'depth grammar' and invent models of language games. Thus, philosophers sometimes wish for a notation which can stress the difference among expressions more explicitly than ordinary language does. Mental cramp is loosened by these notations. Wittgenstein is here using 'notation' to mean any form of language whether natural or devised. To this argument, one might say, quite so, it is entirely desirable not to be mentally paralysed by forms of language especially if such forms embody false "pictures" or "theories", but at the same time one wonders how such an approach to ordinary language can be squared with the belief that it is "all right".

Wittgenstein seems to wish to have things *both* ways. On the one hand, from his theory that the meaning of a word is its use, it follows that however any word is used, the usage or usages are perfectly correct together with whatever theoretical implications such uses might involve. On the other hand, Wittgenstein is highly critical of many of the theoretical overtones or implications of ordinary language, and this means that everything is *not* in order; that words are often used in such a way as to convey misleading, even false ideas. It is hard to believe that Wittgenstein was unaware of this dilemma but he was clearly unable to resolve it. To escape it, he would have had to abandon one of the alternatives outlined above and this he was certainly not prepared to do. He clings to both positions. Hence it is small wonder that his writings manifest a certain 'tension' and even at times incoherence. He was led to two mutually exclusive possibilities which he attempts to reconcile only to fall into inconsistency. For consistency, he would either have had to adopt an unambiguously critical attitude towards ordinary language, or would have had to be prepared to accept its theoretical implications. If he adopted the former alternative, however, he could hardly have argued that the investigation of ordinary language was *the* most fruitful method for the philosopher to employ. Instead of this, however, he claims that his procedure is *descriptive* only, not realising, apparently, that if this were taken at its face value it might be taken to mean that he was only interestd in words for their own sake and in describing just how they are used without any particular theoretical purpose in mind. Wittgenstein was, however, clearly aware that he was not concerning himself with merely verbal questions.

Wittgenstein's procedure shows itself to be 'critically' descriptive to a high degree. He points out that "every particular notation stresses some particular point of view".[18] The phrase 'point of view' is to be especially noted. It suggests that behind usage is something else – a point of view, a theoretical background. If ordinary ways of speaking embody points of view, or theoretical contents of which Wittgenstein was critical, then his invention of new notations embody still further points of view. If a philosopher is persuaded to alter the formulation of his problems this can hardly be done unless we substitute new metaphysical presuppositions in place of the old ones. To criticise one point of view means necessarily to adopt another. It is, however, the point of view which makes a description a philosophical one. Ironically Wittgenstein's own practice makes it clear that, despite the most strenuous efforts, no philosophy can confine itself to the presentation of exemplary reminders. The purpose of assembling reminders is to correct a mistaken analogy and to do this is inevitably to suggest an alternative one. If *Philosophical Investigations* had been merely an album of accepted uses of words, it would not have had the large and generally illuminating influence that it has had.

Moreover, Wittgenstein often says philosophy does not interfere in the working of language; it leaves everything as it is. But is it really the case? Does philosophy leave everything as it is? Just as photography does not leave everything as it is even though it claims that it is faithful copy of it, so is philosophical description. Bombrough says just as "camera changes nothing, even when we can at the same time say that it distorts and garbles and manages the things to which it makes no difference",[19] similarly history, archaeology and photography do not leave things as it is. Perhaps physics and chemistry do not change what they study; but they change many other things. They produce new compounds unknown to nature such as bombs and television. Wittgenstein's philosophy does change ideas about the things and attitudes towards philosophy. His philosophy is certainly a 'radical philosophy'.[20] Descriptive philosophy changes philosopher's perspectives on life, thought and society. Once again we dare to ask does philosophy leave everything as it is? It does not: it clears minds, exposes fallacies and detects insincerities.

In order to make the working of language clearer, Wittgenstein, however, makes use of certain artificial devices by means of which simple patterns of linguistic activity can be exhibited in isolation. These, he calls language games *(Sprachspiel)*. For Wittgenstein the notion of language game serves a number of functions. In some cases he takes it as a simplified model of language, while in others he treats it as a tool to be used in the analysis of complex and a many sided aspects of ordinary language. Wittgenstein applies the term 'language-game' not only to these artificial examples but also to any integrated set of usages forming a complex within the body of a natural language. A natural language is a nexus of such game. In this sense telling the time or making a joke is a language game. A longish list of language games is given in the *Philosophical Investigations.* It includes obeying and giving orders, describing the appearance of objects, giving measurements, constructing an object, reporting an event, testing a hypothesis, presenting the results of experiments in tables and diagrams, making up stories, acting plays, guessing, translating from one language into another, thanking, cursing, greeting and praying, also the language games which include descriptions of physical objects and the description of sense-impressions etc. There are language games, simple and complicated, natural and artificial. A new language game can come into existence and others become obsolete and get forgotten. Wittgenstein says, in *On Certainty,* "a language-game does change with time".[21] 'Sense-data' language is an example of a new language game.

Language games are fundamental "units of sense". They are absolute starting points and are treated as "primary things". Since language games provide only ways of speaking, there is no way of making sense outside them. Language games are logical preconditions. The whole idea of language games arises out of a certain way of looking at phenomena, at language. Wittgenstein speaks of language games as axes, river-beds, scaffoldings and hinges of our using language. The meaning of a word is precisely its role in a particular game. The most common form of philosophical non-sense arises not when a word is being used outside any language-game but when it is used in a language-game other than the one appropriate to it. So it is important to know where one language game ends and another begins. But Wittgenstein is of no help here. One is tempted to ask what are the common characteristics of language-games which differentiate one from other language game. To ask this question means to ask for the hidden essence of one particular language game. Wittgenstein says that it is precisely this type of thinking which is the source of philosophical problems. The errors behind the traditional search for essences have arisen from the mistaken notion that only sharply defined concepts are complete or useful. Languages, for the later Wittgenstein, do not have one essence. Language games are not intended to show us the essence of language. But in them "we see a complicated network of similarities over-lapping and criss-crossing, sometimes overall similarities, sometimes similarities of detail".[22] Language is like a family and language games have only a family resemblance.

Language-games are simple patterns of language. Regarding this Wittgenstein says "These are ways of using signs simpler than those in which we use the signs of our highly complicated everyday language. Language-games are the forms of language with which a child begins to make use of words".[23] The child learns simple language and gradually in course of time he becomes aware of more complicated language. The language we use is not actually as simple as the language of the child, or of primitive people. Wittgenstein, in fact, thinks philosophers committed errors because they wrongly thought our language was simple whereas it is highly complicated. For Wittgenstein, ordinary language is constructed out of these primitive language games. The primitive language used by a tribe is simple and faultless and this language provides the base of developed everyday language. Regarding language games Wittgenstein says, "When we look at such simple forms of language the mental mist which seems to enshroud our ordinary use of language disappears. We see activities, reactions, which are clear-cut and transparent. On the other hand, we recognise in these simple processes forms of language not separated by a break from our more complicated ones. We see that we can build up the complicated forms from the primitive ones by gradually adding new forms".[24] Ordinary language is made out of primitive language i.e. out of simple language games. Our language is in a way a system made out of simple language games.[25]

Since language games are simple forms of language, there is no chance of error at this level. In fact whenever philosophical problems arise philosophers should refer back to primitive language. Wittgenstein says, "If we want to study the problems of truth and falsehood, of the agreement and disagreement of propositions with reality, . . . we shall with great advantage look at primitive forms of language in which these forms of thinking appear without the confusing background of highly complicated processes of thought".[26] For here we see activities and restrictions which are clearest and transparent. In *Remarks on the Foundation of Mathematics,* also Wittgenstein says "When we do philosophy we are like savages, primitive people, who hear the expressions of civilised men, put a false interpretation on them, and then draw queer conclusions from it".[27] In this way language in Wittgenstein's later philosophy is recognised to have its roots in primitive life. Our language games are an extension of primitive behaviours.

The key term here is the word 'primitive' which, in a sense, replaces the word *simple* of the *Tractatus* in the *Blue Book.* A language game is simple and can be compared with the elementary proposition of the *Tractatus.* Just as in the *Tractatus,* the system of language as well as reality cannot be understood without the elementary proposition similarly in the *Blue Book* actual language cannot be understood without language games and also *things* cannot be known without language games because we identify things only through language. In primitive society, primitive language is a system of communication. If someone visits a tribal society and observes the use of signs in their language this is nothing but tracing "the natural history of the tribe." In Wittgenstein's later works, ordinary language is not replaced by new language but is analysed in terms of primitive language. The notion of a simple still lingers on. Wittgenstein's description of language games and activities with which they are connected, however, makes them sound suspiciously mechanical and stereotyped, remarkably free from the improvisations which mark most of our practical activities and the talk they involve.[28] Wittgenstein's description in the *Blue Book* does suggest that language-games are analogous to ideal language in that they are only pure forms of language, 'clearcut' and transparent as he puts it, without the confusing background of thought process which accompany a fully developed language. But he was still thinking in terms of language as a system.

In the *Philosophical Investigations,* Wittgenstein speaks of language-games as the models according to which our actual language is composed although he still retains the primitive language concept of the *Blue Book.* Regarding language-games as models, Wittgenstein says, "we can avoid ineptness or emptiness in our assertions only by presenting the model as what it is, as an object of comparison . . . as a measuring rod".[29] Moreover, in his last work, *On Certainity,* Wittgenstein has confessed, "Not that I could describe the system of these convictions. Yet my convictions do form a system, a structure".[30] Further he says "Our knowledge forms an enormous system. And only within this system has a particular bit the value we give it".[31] It is true that he did accept a system of evidence and varification, of empirical judgements and assumptions and of language games. Yet these systems are by no means speculative. The acceptance of any kind of system nevertheless does make a move away from the piecemeal method even though it is not speculative in character.

The language-game is an analytical tool which he uses to elucidate ordinary language. But this device does not leave things as they are for it certainly interferes in the working of everyday language. It suggests that the ordinary use of language is not safe for philosophy and philosophers should instead probe at a deeper level i.e. at the level of language-games. He mentioned 'language-games' as models in which words function other than normally do. If, for any reason, the study of actual usage does not yield the desired result, that is, if standards of expression are too fixed, or if the way they are used suggests certain 'pictures' or theories which Wittgenstein finds questionable, then he does not hesitate to invent new 'grammar' or new uses of words to break the bondage of the old and to place it in a neat model language game. We do not see language as it actually functions or we do not describe language as it ordinarily works but in terms of language games. The device of language-game is a specific way of looking at language. Wittgenstein's later philosophy shows a reluctance to reduce concepts into neat and clear types of uses. And yet his own model of language-games suggests neat and fixed types within which ordinary language functions. Wittgenstein's conception of language game introduces a new style in philosophy. He is constantly looking for something new. A language game is a phrase invented by himself. Just as "A picture held him captive" in the *Tractatus,* with equal force it might be said "a game holds him captive,"[32] in the *Philosophical Investigations.*

Moreover, Wittgenstein assumed in his later works that philosophers made wrong use of language because of analogies and similes. And yet he himself uses series of analogies. He often speaks of "the analogy between language and game". And he also uses the simile of family resemblance. But the analogies used by Wittgenstein in order to elucidate the nature of language are misleading. The analogy of family resemblance, for example, strongly suggests the idea of the one common essence.[33] More unity than 'criss-crossing' and 'overlapping similarities' is needed to explain why we apply the term 'red' to apples and berries and not to white eggs. The analogy of 'games' *explains* (albeit not in a scientific sense of explanation) and does not *describe* the functionings of language. When Wittgenstein used the notion of 'language game', he is, in fact, explaining the nature and functionings of language. In a book with the unusual title *The Meaning of Poetic Metaphor,* Hestor says the use of Metaphor necessarily *explains* a particular phenomenon which could not be otherwise explained correctly with ordinary language. The use of metaphor is necessarily followed by an explanation, giving reasons for using that metaphor. Without some such explanation other people cannot understand its meaning. For example, when Columbus said to the Queen, "The world is like this orange", the Queen asked "What do you mean? Is the world orange in colour?" Columbus thus had to provide a further explanation for his use of the word 'orange'. He said, I meant the world is like the orange in that both have a spherical shape.[34] Analogies or metaphors are used to explain the nature of particular phenomena and Wittgenstein is no exception to this. Stephen Pepper argues that it is not in science that 'cousins of poetic metaphor' function, but that the essence of metaphysics is to expand the implication of its chosen "root metaphors".[35] Metaphor or analogy is an image-laden, implicitly full form of language. The user of metaphor has a certain image in his mind which he expresses in terms of metaphor.

The question arises why Wittgenstein should have introduced the device of language-games. The answer is that he thought language is an activity, a rule-governed activity. Anyone who participates in a game has to abide by certain rules. The rules which govern a language-game, however, are not necessarily unbreakable or capable of covering every possible move once and for all. Rules are rather models of established practices in society. The use of an expression should conform to rules. We use language in accordance with rules but we are not always *consciously* following rules in the strict sense as is done in mathematics and natural sciences. Those who look for strict rules are in fact looking for something on the analogy of calculi. People do not, in general, use language according to strict rules. We do not think of rule of usage while speaking and, moreover, we normally cannot cite any if we are asked to do so.

The stress is on agreed *common practice* in the use of expressions and this carries with it, in cases where it is appropriate to speak of criteria, the existence of agreed *common criteria* for their application. Rules are like customs, signposts for Wittgenstein. They are neither correct nor incorrect. The rule in Wittgenstein is a description or a part of a description of what we do and what we expect others to do. A rule is a stable custom which functions overtly in a game. Inner criteria do not function in a public language game. A language with private rules would not be a language. This is perhaps why Wittgenstein rules out the possibility of private language and private criteria. The use of a sign is shaped and given significance by what he called 'natural history'. It is not possible that there should have been only one occasion on which an order was given, a promise made, a question asked, a debt procured, or a game played. Following a rule, making a promise, giving an order are customs, practices and institutions.

On Wittgenstein's account, only in circumstances where a radically different kind of life obtains could we practise different rules. We can't, of course, seriously envisage such alternatives to our conceptual system; our natural history prevents it. Had our natural history been different our ways of counting and calculating would have been different. It is not merely by decision that we adopt these rules but our adoption of rules is based on the natural history of mankind. Wittgenstein's account of rules as rule – governed activity along with the account of rules as not needing justification has a certain appeal. But things are not so simple. It is not enough to point to the existence of concrete expressions of rules and to the facts of natural human history as the background of customary operations which function as paradigms. What is to be explained is how and when I follow a rule. We want to be shown how rule provide either a cause or a reason for my action. Though we cannot say that our behaviour is being caused by rules, still, we may feel, what is to be guided by a rule is a certain experience or mental state; a feeling of being guided, a feeling that one is acting because of rules.

One of the most important things in Wittgenstein's philosophy is his stress that language is a part of community activity, a way of living in society. In fact, like eating and walking, speaking is also an activity, a form of life. In other words "to imagine a language means to imagine a form of life".[36] Forms of life are established patterns of action shared by people of a particular time and culture. Any action which is established as belonging to a group and which has common meaning shared by members of that group and thus any activity which is regularised and institutionalized is a form of life. The use of language is ultimately referred to forms of life by Wittgenstein in the *Philosophical Investigations.* This is the ultimate terminus of inquiry. 'Forms of life' are presupposed by the conceptual structures of language. This is the essential 'framework' in which our language functions. The "common behaviour of mankind" constitutes "system of reference" for interpreting language. Speaking or using a language presup poses a complete background of activities, habits and mutual understandings without which the sound produced would be no more than meaningless noises. The detailed investigations of concepts such as name, thought, rule, led him to believe that the base on which language rests, the framework into which it fits, is provided not by a structure of unchanging atoms but by a shifting pattern of 'form of life' based on a common human nature. To imagine a language means to imagine a culture and when human beings agree in language they actually agree in their form of life.[37] Unlike most philosophers of his day Wittgenstein says, "we don't start from certain words but from certain occasions or activities".[38] Forms of life are intelligible settings of language amidst human affairs. Wittgenstein says "it is our *acting,* which lies at the bottom of the language-game".[39] Language games within which words alone have meaning, are in fact, forms of life, the modes of activity governed by systems of rules. A language game in one of its uses is thus a simplified model embedded in a form of life, a clear instance of some characteristic use of language in a typical life situation. Descriptive philosophy takes a turn towards what is original, natural and native. Form of life and language are tied up with each other and are thus interdependent.

Behind man's language and so behind his philosophy, there lies the history of man. Forms of life refer to the stories that are behind words and which illuminate the rules by which words acquire their meaning. Wittgenstein is not in *Philosophical Investigations* interested in tracing the very general facts behind language. That would be to do natural science. The facts in which Wittgenstein is interested lie incorporated in human history. Wittgenstein, however, is not concerned with this, but with forms of life and this means that Wittgenstein is concerned with meaning and not with facts. Forms of life are patterns of meaningful actions. Just as forms of objects are possibilities of meaning in the *Tractatus,* similarly forms of life are possibilities of meaning in *Philosophical Investigations.* What holds language games and forms of life together is not rules, but a still wider *context* presupposed by both of them, the content of everyday life and everyday certainty which Wittgenstein discusses in his last book *On Certainty.* This wider context is not something we "know", but is rather the framework in terms of which our knowing takes place.

The conclusion follows that the model of language games

is based on something even more foundational, that is, forms of life. It is this that provides the solid basis for language games. In Wittgenstein's own language "forms of life" clearly play the role of a metaphysical ultimate in terms of which the description is to be understood. They are given as an indubitable basis, a rock of certainty, like the Cartesian *Cogito.* It seems that the conception of philosophy as description logically requires completion in the idea of something of this sort. With out some such anchorage description would be utterly devoid of philosophical import. Only by postulating an ultimate factuality, the conception of philosophy as description makes any sense.

References

1. L. Wittgenstein, *Philosophical Investigations,* para 109.
2. L. Wittgenstein, *Ibid.,* para 126.
3. *Ibid.,* para 109.
4. *Ibid.,* para 109.
5. *Ibid.,* para 132.
6. *Cf.* G.A. Paul, "Wittgenstein", *The Revolution in Philosophy,* ed. by A.J. Ayer etc., p. 95
7. *Cf.* David Pole, *The Later Philosophy of Wittgenstein,* pp. 85-86.
8. The years Wittgenstein spent in teaching elementary school children may be considered one of the most decisive factors in the shaping of his later philosophy. The reality of teaching children how to read, write and the experience of compiling a dictionary for elementary schools must have contributed to Wittgenstein's later philosophy.
9. L. Wittgenstein, *Philosophical Investigations,* para 11.
10. *Ibid.,* para 421.

11. L. Wittgenstein, *Blue Book,* p. 43.

12. Wittgenstein, *Philosophical Grammar,* p. 184.

13 *Ibid.,* p 60.

14 L. Wittgenstein, *Philosophical Investigations,* Sec. 122.

15. *Ibid.,* para 664.

16. *Ibid.,* para 224.

17. *Ibid.,* para 126.

18. L. Wittgenstein, *Blue Book,* p. 28.

19. Bombrough, Renford, "Does philosophy leave everything as it is", *The philosophy in Christainity,* p. 225.

20. *Ibid.,* p. 226.

21. L. Wittgenatein, *On Certainty,* para 256.

22. L. Wittgenstein, *Philosophical Investigations,* para 66.

23. L. Wittgenstein, *Blue Book,* p. 17.

24. *Ibid.*

25. In this respect Wittgenstein was influenced by the famous economist Sraffa. A glimpse of Sraffa's positive constribution may be detected in his only published work, *Preclude to a Critique of Economic Theory.* Sraffa starts his investigation of the process of production with an imaginary society, "Let us consider an extremely simple society which produces just enough to maintain itself . . .. Suppose at first that only two commodities are produced and then builds up the more complicated forms by gradually adding new features." (Sraffa, *op.cit.* p. 3). This method, central to Sraffa's investigations is adopted by Wittgenstein in his later works. The important method of imagining and constructing simple and complicated 'language games' seems to be an adaption of Sraffa's method. To this W. Mays ("Recollections of Wittgenstein", *Wittgenstein Man and His Philosophy* ed. by K.T. Fann page 83) says that Wittgenstein uses the method of 'speculative anthropology'.

26. Wittgenstein, L. *Blue Book,* p. 17

27. Wittgenstein, L. *Remarks on the Foundation of Mathematics,* Eng. tr. by G.E.M. Anscombe, para 125.

28. *Cf.* Rush Rhees; "Wittgenstein's Builders", *Proceedings of the Aristotelian*

Society, 1959, Vol. 60, pp. 171-86.

29. L. Wittgenstein, *Philosophical Investigations,* para 131.

30. L. Wittgenstein, *On Certainty,* para 162.

31. *Ibid.*, para 410.

32. Helen Hervey, "The Problem of Model Language-Game in Wittgenstein's Later Philosophy", *Philosophy,* 1961, Vol. 36, p. 333.

33. *Cf.* R. Bombrough "Universals and Family Resemblances", *Proceedings of the Aristotelian Society,* 1960-61, Vol. 61, pp. 207-22.

34. Cf. Marcus B. Hester, *The Meaning of Poetic Metaphor,* p. 23.

35. *Cf.* Stephen C. Pepper, *World Hypotheses : A Study in Evidence;* pp. 84-115.

36. L. Wittgenstein, *Philosophical Investigations,* p. 19.

37. *Ibid.*, para 241.

38. L. Wittgenstein, *Lectures and Conversations on Aesthetics, Psychology and Religious Believer,* ed. by C. Barrett, para 5.

39. L. Wittgenstein, *On Certainity,* p. 201.

4

Description in Husserl's Philosophy

HUSSERL, like Wittgenstein, says the philosophers' "authentic task is of pure description". His phenomenology is "a *pure descriptive* discipline which studies the whole field of pure transcendental consciousness in the light of pure intuition."[1] However, the problem of description in Husserl arises in a certain context. The nature of the philosophical discipline as he conceives it, consequently, is of a different type. The descriptive programme is no longer a question of the use and usage of language. It deals with the description of the essential structures of pure experiences, pure consciousness.

The emphasis on the descriptive programme, however, is not found in Husserl's early writings. His earliest philosophical problem was the logic of mathematics. In *Philosophy of Arithmetic* Husserl's aim was to clarify the basic *presuppositions* of mathematics. He wanted to clarify what he called the 'origin' of the concept of number. In *Logical Investigations,* too, Husserl was interested in the foundation of mathematics and the philosophy of logic. But soon he realised that "the theoretical framework of the mathematical disciplines and all the theorems which develop within it cannot be of any service".[2] The "descriptive science of Essential Being belongs in fact to a *main class of eidetic science wholly other* than that to which the mathematical sciences belong".[3] For "to establish such a thing as a mathematics of phenomena, may mislead . . . the very idea of phenomenology".[4]

Husserl became interested in the descriptive programme only in the last phase of the first decade of the century. In the five lectures delivered in Gottingen in 1907, he used the descriptive method for the first time. Later in 1913 in the *Ideas,* which holds a special place in the history of philosophy because of its introduction of a new philosophical method, he fully explained the scope of the descriptive programme. However, in later years Husserl drifted from this programme and became involved in the 'constitution' of the world. His interest shifted from the 'description' to the 'constitution' of the world. In the later writings, the concept of life-world becomes more important, and interestingly this concept resembles that of Wittgenstein's "forms of life". Both of them refer to a more practical and historical horizon which provides the contextual framework for the analysis of meaning, and this in spite of the general lack of interest of each, in their early work, in historicity.

We are here dealing with this intermediate period of Husserl's academic career mainly for two reasons; firstly, his descriptive philosophy is propounded in this period; and, secondly, his claim to importance in philosophy arises out of his philosophical standpoint in this particular period. Existentialists, as well as Max Scheler, were greatly influenced by his descriptive philosophy and utilised it for their own purposes.

Since Husserl is concerned with the nature of experience and its essential structures, his descriptive philosophy can be sharply distinguished from that of the practitioners of linguistic analysis. The objects of experience, for Husserl, are neither mental in a subjectivistic sense nor do they have independent existence. They have a special status of their own. For scientists objects exist independently and for subjective idealists objects exist in the mind. But for Hussserl the object of experiences 'exist' in yet another way. The problem of description in Husserl's philosophy arises in the context of his own special understanding of what these "objects" are.

Husserl's descriptive philosophy is tied up with his aim of making philosophy a rigorous science. The ideal of a descriptively founded philosophy may be held up and a final definition of what he would like to achieve if he adopts the scientific ideal in philosophy. This is not to say, however, that Husserl's own method of descriptive analysis within the limits of what he called "transcendental subjectivity" was adequate for all philosophical purposes. It was not. But it is the notion of what a rigorous philosophy would involve that provides the framework for his conception of descriptive philosophy.

Descriptive phenomenology is solely concerned with how the phenomena, the things themselves, are presented in pure consciousness. His search is not for whether the thing is. He searches for how the thing presents to us, how the phenomena appear. Husserl's main question in philosophy is 'How is a world given to us?' His aim thus is to describe the world just as it presents itself to us, and to describe the forms of consciousness in which this presentation is actualized. In pure description, the thing is not presented to the senses but to pure intuition. Description enables us to avoid both traditional metaphysical systems as well as referential questions about the physical world.

The first requirement for his descriptive philosophy is to adopt the reflective attitude. Husserl appeals for a radical attitude, a new way of looking at things. We must look at the world with "new eyes". Philosophy needs an entirely new point of departure and an entirely new method which will not concern itself with the natural world. What is this method? Phenomenological investigation, for Husserl, is carried out in a framework in which the epoche is constantly operative. The epoche gives "*a new way of looking at* things, . . . one that contrasts *at every point* with the natural attitude of experience and thought".[5] Husserl characterized his method as a revolution in the natural way of thinking. The epoche is meant to establish a certain theoretical *ingenuousness* which does not have the drawbacks of the naive natural attitude. It brings about a change in our attitude. It is an awakening from the 'dogmatic slumber' of the mundane ontology of the everyday world into the questioning search for truth. This liberates philosophers from the naive, universal belief in the reality of the "natural world" through "bracketing" the operative power of latency, concealment, misunderstanding and deception. Descriptive phenomenology is thus a 'critique of mundanity'. To be radical means thus to question all concepts, to indicate the point that none is sufficiently familiar for us to take it for granted. It is a technique aimed at assuring that we have a presuppositionless philosophy.

Husserl insists on the necessity of first philosophy although he rejects traditional metaphysics. The original spirit of the phenomenological programme is the clarification of meanings by following the ideal of pure, presuppositionless description beyond all interpretation, justification, idealization and theory formation. Description is a methodology of philosophy to clarify and determine the meaning of the phenomena, to carry out an elucidatory analysis of them. Husserl believes the problem for the critique of knowledge is to locate the absolutely bare, presuppositionless data on which to build the whole of knowledge; more precisely the problem is to intuit the essence of knowledge and thereby to "see" how valid cognition is an unquestionable fact. Husserl's slogan is 'let experience tell its own tale'. From Descartes he has followed the methodical principle "claim only what you can see clearly". Description is first person's inquiry instead of third person's inquiry.

Husserl primary intention is thus to establish the primacy of the 'given'. Given not so much in the sense of the data in our naively daytoday immediacy but as those given through higher level of reflection. Phenomenological reflection detaches itself from the natural attitude *(natürliche Einstellung)* loaded with too many prejudices. This, it does in order to be able to describe the pure given without favouring the one at the cost of the other. Phenomenological reflection is something which one has to cultivate. It is an accomplishment.

The radicality of the stance puts the ordinary world within brackets and leads to a new world of pure consciousness.

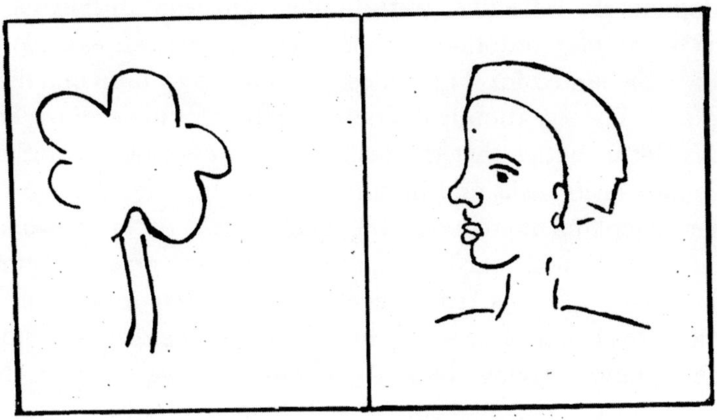

First person's inquiry

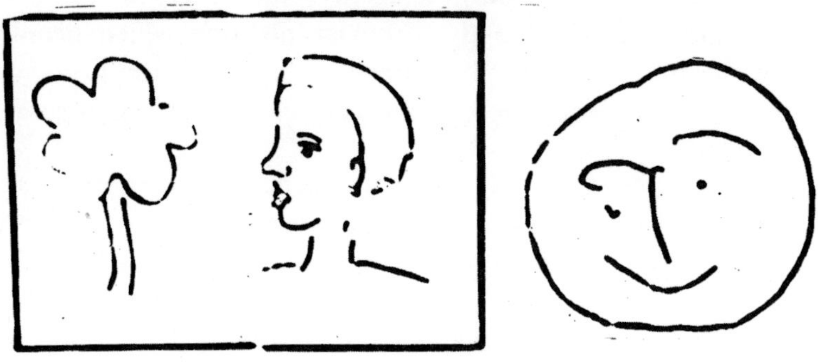

Third person's inquiry

The phenomenological reduction is a methodological device which takes us to the region of pure data, to pure consciousness. "If we wish to construct a phenomenology as a *pure descriptive theory of the essential nature of the immanent formations of Consciousness* -- we must exclude from this limited field everything that is transcendently individual, -- also *all* the *transcendent essences,* whose logical position lies rather in the theory of the essential nature of the relevant transcendent objectivities".[6]

The subject-matter of pure description in fact is hidden from the ordinary point of view[7] and made evident by only adopting the reflective attitude. For Wittgenstein language, the object of description, is there, 'lying before our eyes'. It is not to be hunted for. The philosophers just pick it up and describe it. The situation is different in Husserl's philosophy. He says "let us notice that the task of phenomenology, or rather the area of its tasks and inquiries, is no such trivial things as merely looking, merely opening, one's eyes".[8] A "full personal transformation of man" is required in order to grasp the pure phenomena. This is reminiscent of Plato's requirement of a complete change or *metabasis* in order to see the reality behind the shadow. Leaving the straightforward, naive attitude, the philosopher is to take a critical, detached and reflective stand. Phenomenology signifies an *attitude* of thought. The concept of attitude *(Einstellung)* plays a decisive role in Husserl. It is a question of modifying the ordinary attitude which people assume towards their environment. Common sense becomes the *arriere-garde* of philosophy instead of being its *avant-garde.*

The necessary outcome of this change is that every thesis related to externality must be disconnected and put into brackets. Regarding the natural world Husserl says, *"we set it as it were "out of action"*, we *"disconnect it", "bracket it"*.[9] But Husserl does not deny the existence of the natural world, for to deny existence is also to take a stand with respect to the world. Moreover, such negations or doubts presuppose a natural world. Husserl simply puts existentiality out of action. "I do *not* then *deny* this "world", as though I were a sophist, *I do not doubt that it is there* as though I were a sceptic; but I use the "phenomenological" Eπox n, which *completely bars me from using any judgement that concerns spatio-temporal existence (Desein)"*.[10] The bracketed matter is not wiped off from the phenomenological slate, but only bracketed. To the objective world we give a "different value". The empirical ego also goes within brackets along with the spatio-temporal world.

One of the main reasons for suspension of the thesis of the existence of the ordinary world is that it implies naturalism, and since Husserl's philosophy is transcendental it is essentially non-naturalistic and non-objectivistic. The epoche is a necessary device for preserving methodological purity and for preventing a slipping back into the follies of naturalism. Husserl's anti-naturalism includes an attack on many doctrines and methods which would not normally be considered 'naturalistic' but which from Husserl's point of view fail to give absolute truths. Naturalists, positivists, historicists and scientists are obsessed with the facts, and their argumentations are inevitably relativistic. Husserl drafted an ambitious and comprehensive programme for a logical investigation that was to penetrate the empirical and factual world so as ultimately to leave it behind in quest of the discovery of "eternal" and evident validity. By "eternal" he meant that such validity would not be affected by changes in the world of facts and so would stand apart from human history.

After epoche what are we left with? Or in other words, after bracketing the world what do we have? After changing attitude towards the physical world, Husserl is ready for first reduction i.e. phenomenological reduction. Here one is no longer concerned about what may or may not exist, but about the structure of the phenomena as such. One has to analyse how phenomena present themselves, how they are defined in consciousness. What lies behind the phenomena is no longer of interest; what is important is how they behave in the field of pure consciousness, how they present themselves "immanently". Through phenomenological reduction Husserl bracketed the reality including its ontological claims, and regarded it as a mere field of phenomena. Within the phenomenological reduction the "thing", viewed not as a bit of "reality", but as a certain structure, as a phenomena. Phenomenology is interested in describing the pure phenomena as they appear in consciousness. There is no "being behind the phenomena". The phenomenologist is concerned with how the objects appear rather than how objects exist. The interest is in meaning rather than in ontology.

But whose consciousness Husserl is talking about or what type of consciousness Husserl has in mind? Here he performs second reduction i.e. the transcendental reduction. Husserl bracketed himself, empirical "I", factual and individual consciousness so as to lay open to view the structural conditions. In place of 'individual' consciousness, structure of general consciousness becomes focus of discussion. This reduction is for myself, to see my consciousness as at once a universal phenomenon of consciousness of the world and self-consciousness. Once the individual particularities of consciousness is reduced, one is in the realm of absolute - the inter-subjective community of consciousness. In Husserl's phenomenology consciousness is neither defined psychologically (as the consciousness of an individual) nor metaphysically (as a higher, superhuman consciousness existing in itself such as Hegel's *Geist*) but in a transcendental way.

Transcendental here indicates pure consciousness in which "meanings" disclose themselves. The residum of reductions is pure structure of consciousness or the pure structures of experiences. Husserl's aim is to describe this structure. The secret of meaning is hidden in the structure of consciousness of *Ego - Cogito - Cogitatum.* The word "Absolute" is never applicable to something real or something existing, but to that which cannot be further reduced. That is why Husserl treats this immenent, non-empirical consciousness as absolute because in principle it needs no other matter for its own existence.

Transcendental ego stands outside the structure of reduced consciousness as the guarantee of unity in the objects of thought. Transcendental ego is the ultimate guarantee of the signifying powers of that inner time through which alone the synthesis of the meaning is achieved. The realm of the reduced consciousness over which Transcendental Ego presides has no connection with the reality of common existence. Husserl says "between the meanings of consciousness and reality yawns a veritable abyss".

The following diagram may explain his philosophy better.

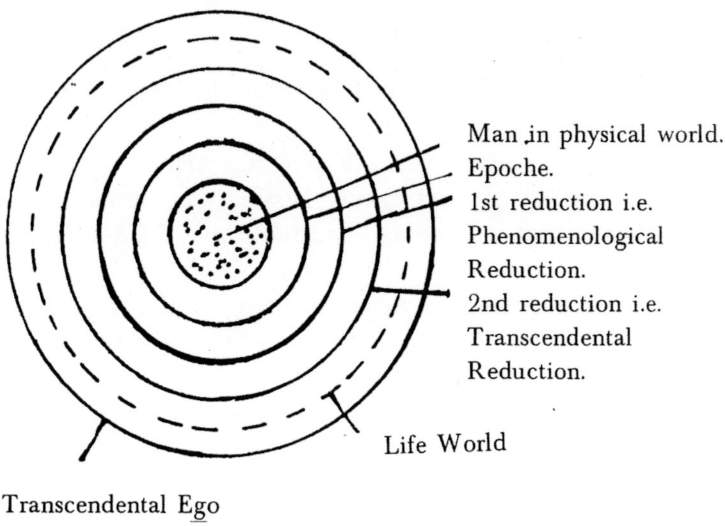

The outcome of the epoche and the transcendental phenomenological reductive method is an awareness of and an ability to describe the *genuine sense* of the world, the sense which is constantly being by-passed by the attempts of philosophers to reduce it to some simple scheme or other, such as that of "naturalism". In the *Cartesian Meditations* Husserl says, "phenomenological explication does nothing but *explicate the sense the world has for all prior to any philosophizing . . . a sense which philosophy can uncover but never alter*".[11] With the discovery and explication of the concept of the life-world Husserl feels that he has finally arrived at the fulfilment of this project. The genuine or most fundamental sense of the world, the sense that underlies all interpretations of its objects is the ground which makes phenomenological description possible.

Husserl's method is metaphysically neutral. It is true, he is prepared to speak of a metaphysics but only as a "prima philosophia",[12] a consideration of reality prior to all new inventions and discoveries and not in the sense of a "historically degenerated metaphysics". It is meaningless to speak, as the traditional metaphysics does, of a world in itself which is destitute of meaning.

The field that is opened up after the execution of the reduction is neither "psychologistic nor metaphysical"; it is "transcendental". Reduction, is thus not merely a technique without any further and deeper mission. It permits us to go beyond all psychologism and relativism to a realm of apodictic evidence. The discovery of the most original field of experience is what reduction aims at. Things unfold themselves within the scope of transcendental reduction. And there we are concerned with description of phenomena, that is to say, with structures of consciousness through which their descriptions can come about. The reduction enables him to describe "things" without prejudice, that is to say, phenomena as they appear. The question of what *'exists'* is no longer asked. We are concerned solely with "meanings" which are given independently of all explanation, whether psychological or philosophical. This saves philosophers from construction and theorization both of which are ruled out in the phenomenological programme. The redical philosopher does not construct in order to show how certain things are possible if others are assumed, but elucidates meanings. Radical philosophy "explicates" and "clarifies". Husserl says, "phenomenological explication is nothing like 'metaphysical construction'; and it is neither overtly nor covertly a theorising with adopted presuppositions - drawn from the historical metaphysical tradition".[13] Husserl is not concerned with concepts but with the structures of consciousness. The reductive method gives us a "new" world, a "live" world. Phenomenology, in virtue of its radical reflection or phenomenological reduction is a special way of looking at the world, namely, as *meant,* that is, by reference to intentional consciousness.

Up to now our discussion reveals Husserl's philosophy as radically revolutionary and the revolution was intended to be an on-going one in the sense that the philosopher constantly used to shed assumptions. But it is not easy to perform the reduction and to remain faithful to it. Husserl admits, "It takes unusual consistency and energy of thought to remain firm and not to fall back into the traditional ways of thinking, to really take hold of the new, without falling into such tempting relapses".[14] Mental effort is required not only to achieve the phenomenological reduction but also to stick to it, to avoid "falling back" into the natural attitude. The image of falling, of a gravitational pull on consciousness, corresponds to Husserl's use of the term "natural" in the expression "natural attitude". To fall is to lapse into.

A question naturally arises, why should we need to perform the reduction. Why does Husserl suspend belief in the natural world? It is rather strange that in the twentieth century, when the emphasis is on the commonsense world, Husserl should adopt a contrary approach. What made Husserl go against the contemporary trend? It is almost as if in order to gain the world he must first lose it. Also keeping the description pure necessitates that the philosopher must disregard the natural world. Husserl is searching for the pure datum which can be grasped only after detaching it from this world. Without the redicalization of the phenomenological reduction, any description of and by consciousness would be imcomplete, and it would not accomplish the discovery of transcendental consciousness in its full range of powers and complexity.

Phenomenology is not averse to the field of our concrete experiences. Rather it opens up a way to 'live' worlds and to seeing them more intimately. But critics think that Husserl's philosophy is a "flight from reality" to alleged higher certainties. Van Peursen rejects Husserl's reduction as a mystical terminology of "leaving" the natural world. Probably because of this Husserl in his later works has taken the problem of existence of the world in a different perspective. But then he gradually drifted from the descriptive programme and became more interested in the 'pre-scientific' world. However, this interest in the material world at the end of his philosophical career, is not a new phenomenon in the history of philosophy. Every important thinker, including Russell and Wittgenstein, returned to the ordinary world only after a philosophical detour. This going round about is useful in the sense that it elucidates and clarifies many philosophical issues.

Husserl claims that through the methodological procedure of reduction nothing has been lost. The whole sphere of Absolute Being has been won. The "phenomenological epoche lays open to me, (the meditating philosopher) *an infinite realm of being of a new kind . . .*"[15]. It is a world of pure consciousness. Consciousness is like an infinite stream for him, a "stream of experience". It is immediately present to the phenomenologist. "We move in the field of pure phenomena. But why do I say *field?* It is more nearly a *Heraclitean flux of phenomena.*"[16] Husserl's aim is to analyse and describe the essential structures of pure experiences. His method is intentional analysis in its descriptive phenomenological dimension. He analyzes and describes conscious acts and their contents. Phenomenological analysis is surely meaning-analysis which is concerned with processes of experience. His *modus operandi* becomes analysis by description. In other words, describing includes the practice of analysing the activity of reflection.

A phenomenological method is neither deductive nor inductive, but consists in pointing to what is 'given' and *elucidating* it. It fixes its gaze directly upon whatever is presented to consciousness. No systems of mediated deductions are built up, for outside the formal theory of deductive systems by iteslf generally cannot function as an instrument of discovery. Husserl is not one of those philosophers who seek to reform our thought about the world. Rather he is content to describe that thought.

The aim of analysis for Husserl, and here he is one with other analytical philosophers, is to clarify. But unlike the modern linguistic analytical philosophers, Husserl analyses the essential structures of *experiences* and *consciousness.* The modern Anglo-American philosophers, on the other hand, are interested in the analysis of *language* and in its logical structure. By "analysis they (the analytic philosophers) meant something which, whatever precise description of it they chose, at least involved the attempt to rewrite in different and in some way more appropriate terms those statements which they found philosophically puzzling".[17] The analysis amounts actually to a construction of new expressions rather than a study of the component parts of the original ones. By contrast phenomenological analysis is not primarily concerned with linguistic expressions. It only analyses the phenomenon within the region of immanent experiences and not the expressions that refer to them. Husserl analyses the intentional structures of experiences. Intentional analysis is something totally different from analysis in the usual sense. Intentional analysis uncovers the activities and potentialities in which objects are constituted as units of senses.[18] His reflective analysis renders explicit what is implicit or makes overt what was hidden in our experiences. The analysis consists in tracing those constitutive phenomena which are the primary data of our knowledge.

Husserl is confronted not with confusions created by the uses of language, but with dogmatism, the dogmatism of the positivists and those who assume the latter are correct. But the positivists apart, Husserl is confronted also with the historicists, Dilthey, for example, and scientists like Galileo, for they too 'behave dogmatically'. Husserl generalized his new concept of philosophy by attacking "naturalism" – the claim that statements in the existing sciences are premises in philosophic argument – and "historicism" – the view that philosophic truths but are relative to historical epoche. Husserl says "Let us, therefore, protect ourselves methodically from those confusions which are too deeply rooted in us, as born dogmatists . . . ."[19] But how can we protect ourselves against dogmatism? Firstly, by putting the natural world, which is the source of confusion, in brackets and, secondly by analysing the experiences to find out what actually is 'given' in them. The aim of Husserl's philosophy is to fight against the 'non-sensical confusions' of dogmatism. Positivists (he is thinking of Mach and Avenarius) are not as radical as they claim to be because in the analysis of experiences they do not go as deep as they should have gone. Though they claim to deal with the 'given', their given is actually loaded with presuppositions and bounded by prejudices.

Husserl's primary aim is to describe and analyzes the essential structure of experiences and consciousness. He finds that every conscious act of experience is intentional and has a dual character. Husserl's object is to give "descriptive analysis of intentional experiences in their essential nature".[20] Intentionality plays a key role in Husserl's descriptive programme. The essential structures of consciousness and of experiences is intentional. "It is intentionality which characterises *consciousness* in the pregnant sense of the term, and justifies us in describing the whole stream of experience as at once a stream of consciousness and unity of *one* consciousness".[21] The 'bucket' concept of consciousness wherein we think of consciousness as a reservoir of 'impressions', 'associations' and 'memories', is replaced by intentionality. Our experience is never wholly determined by the nature of the objects; it is always a product of the interaction between object and subject. Phenomenology thus rejects distinction between subject and object and in its aims at least, is neither subjectivist nor objectivist. The question then arises what is intentionality? It is an inseparable relation between the noetic and noematic aspects of experience. In other words, the act of experience is inseparable relation to the contents of experience. Intentionality is directedness *(Richtung)* of an act of consciousness towards an object *(Gegenstand)*. Every physical phenomenon is characterized by its object; for example, representation is characterized by the object which it represents, such an object is not necessarily something real but it intrinsically qualifies the specific psychic act; for example, the act of imagining, is qualified by its imaginary object. An intentional act may have as its object an existentially mind-dependent entity, for example, the idea of a mermaid, or its object may be something physical; or it may be an impossible thing such as the round square; or its may be something possible but unactualized, such as a golden mountain.

In acts of perception, understanding and the like subject

directs its attention to an "object" (a thing, a mathematical proposition, a remembered events, etc). This is not to say that the object in question is immediately given in such an act.

In place of the thesis that consciousness always *has* an object, he substituted the thesis that consciousness is always *directed* towards an object. This need not be an actual object. He calls it *noema.* Each noema is not only an apparent object or an 'appearance'; it is also a *Sinn,* or rather it *has* a *Sinn,* and separates off a certain *'noematic nucleus'* from the changing *'characters'* that belong to it.

In our consciousness there is a *noemata* of a tree, a cow, a river, colour, texture etc. One analyses each of these noemata in pure consciousness, without referring to any particular tree or cow or river in the external world. When we try to understand any reality that we encounter in the external world there happens to be a two-fold process. Firstly, our consciousness turns its intentionality towards it. Secondly, from the inexhaustible fund of noemata in our consciousness, we compose an appropriate noemata which we presume will fit the externally encountered object or target of our intentionality. This thetic or projecting process is what Husserl calls noesis. This is as if pure consciousness is a computer having an extremely wide range of noemata. At a particular moment of time, an appropriate aspect of that noemata is chosen out of that range. It is clear that the noetic process presupposes the existence of an appropriate noemata already innate in consciousness. This presupposition comes from the Platonic tradition of eidetic essences innate in the mind and from the theory of knowledge and rememberance. But Husserl would deny that source and would insist the presence of the noemata in consciousness is a fact of observation, apodietically self-evident.

Both noemata and noesis are inter-dependent and inseparable; both are eidetic; noema is innate in consciousness; noesis is an intentional act, thetic, directed. Noetic acts are unique formation of consciousness and may not be re-enacted. The noema of consciousness can, however recur and may be recaptured through various noetic acts. For instance a chair in the room. It may be apprehended not only through a variety of spatial perspective i.e. from above, below, from very close, from a great distance, and so on but also from a variety of temporal perspectives. It can be seen in present time, past, remembered, or projected; it can be imagined or can be dreamt. In each and every act of consciousness that aspect of the chair which is perspectively brought into the realm of consciousness forms, the noema, the various acts of consciousness through which it is made available from the noeses. Meaningfulness is dependent on the systematic organization of the noemata. As each noema is a perspective grasp of the chair in the room, so knowledge of the same chair rests on the systematically organized totality of its noemata, a multiplicity of noemata being attributable to the one object in reality.

We are to look at the object as "intended" and "meant". The phenomena, the things, the essences, are not independently given; they are dependent on the acts of consciousness. The objects always belong to consciousness. Every conscious act is 'consciousness of' something. The meaning of an object (a house which I see, an event which I remember etc.) which is discovered in the description of this significant structure and in the bracketing of any ontological claim, this *meaning,* is the object considered according to the manner in which it shows itself. Consciousness and the object of consciousness are inextricably interwoven in any form of appearance whatsoever. Experience is understood in a 'global sense' in which act and content are embraced together. Experiences are 'object-focused.' Husserl's main question is how the objects are given in the very act of consciousness. Now the phenomenological method proceeds entirely through acts in reflection. Reflection is an expression for acts in which the stream of experience with all its manifold phases can be grasped and analysed in the light of its own evidence. In reflection one becomes aware of oneself, and awareness of oneself includes the awareness of the object. Describing the act is at the same time describing its object. Thus Husserl is committed to the description of both noetic and noematic aspects of experience.

Whereas the linguistic analytic philosopher is interested only in the sentence spoken and not the speaker, Husserl describes the polarity of experience. *Cogito* and *Cogitatum* are both manifestations which are being described. Husserl recognises different phenomenological levels within experience. For the analytical philosophers there is, however, just one level of phenomena, i.e., the language. In Husserl's descriptive phenomenology even the most elementary experience has a dual character.

Husserl's main contribution in the history of philosophy lies in his understanding of the way objects are 'given'. The intentional objects are neither physical objects as the scientists and the realists thought, nor mental as the idealists maintained. They are objects of certain signifying intentions. Objects occupy an important place in Husserl's phenomenology. His slogan is "Back to the things themselves". *(Zurüch zu den Sachen selbst)*. His call is for "the things themselves" not for "things in themselves" for the later leads to speculative metaphysics. This adage Husserl advanced in various forms in order to characterize his method and this became a slogan for thinkers of the phenomenological school. The closest Husserl comes in this publication to using the phrase is in *Logical Investigations,* where he asked for not 'mere words' but the "things themselves"[22] and in his manifesto article *Philosophy as Rigorous Science,* where he says "In the epoche of vigorous reaction against Scholasticism the war cry was: 'Away with empty word analysis. We must question things themselves. Back to experience, the seeing, which alone can give to our words sense and rational justification'. Very much to the point".[23] In the same work he further says that research starts "not from philosophies but from the things and from the problems connected with them".[24] It was Heidegger who explicitly asserted that "To the things themselves" was the basic maxim of phenomenology.[25]

'Direct seeing' of essences rules out any possibility of doubt. It also excludes deduction and inference which necessarily lead to speculative metaphysics. What is the nature of this essential 'insight'? It is nothing but pure intuition, "primordial dator intuition" which is the "principle of principles". It is the measure of all truth, and statements which give faithful expressions to their data need fear nothing from the finest arguments. It is a "source of authority . . . for knowledge, that whatever presents itself in "intuition" in primordial forms . . . is simply to be accepted as it gives itself out to be, though only within the limits in which it then presents itself".[26] The importance of intuition is also emphasized in the well known preface to the first volume of *Journal für Philosophie und Phenomenologie,* a yearbook with Husserl as its main editor. "It is not an academic system that binds the *editors* and that ought to be presupposed by all the future editors. Our unity is furnished by the common conviction that only by means of returning to the original sources of intuition and to the insights into essences derived from them can the great traditions of philosophy be intuitively clarified. Then the problems of philosophy can be newly set forth on an intuitive basis and can be solved once and for all".[27] Thus Husserl's method of philosophy is a method of pure intuition. This is what is at the root of his epistemology. Phenomenological intuition constitutes the locus in which so-called phenomenological facts – pure essences – are self-given.

The essences are neither constructed nor inferred, they are revealed in pure intuitive experiences. Husserl's slogan "Back to the things themselves" is meant as an appeal addressed to philosophers to get away from constructions, theories and hypotheses and to see things as they are, 'given' in pure intuition. Phenomenology depends upon our having something directly accessible and ('phenomena') not determined or patterned by assumed constructs. Husserl claims that there is something which is evident to intuition, that is, one simply sees it and need not argue one's way to it. At the level of basic philosophical insight there are not formal proofs, no knock-down arguments, but only admonitions to "look again" (Wittgenstein) or to "get back to things themselves" (Husserl). Husserl advises that philosophers should save themselves from drifting beyond what is immediately 'given'; and he also advises against Occam's razor for he warns "nor are the phenomena to be diminished below what is intuitively given". Only such an approach can prevent dogmatic over-simplifications and disastrous generalisation regardless of whether they come from the speculative or the sceptical wing of philosophy. To skip this stage runs counter to the ideal of philosophy as a universal and at the same time, a rigorous science, the pursuit of which are Husserl's deepest concern.

It seems that Husserl had been strongly impressed by the positivists' emphasis on the immediately given. But his idea of an intuition which reveals the 'given' is very different from that of the positivists. Intuition, which offers things themselves, is contrasted with a simple "representation", whether the latter be actual or non-actual. Husserl is convinced that it is phenomenology and not positivism which is, in the true sense, concerned with what is immediately and directly 'given'. He took the positivists to task for their blunder of equating the 'given' with sense data, 'seeing' with the 'sensible'. Husserl claimed that phenomenologists "are the genuine positivists". Recent interpretation of Husserl also highlights this feature. Mohanty sees in Husserl a positivist doctrine of the fulfilment of the intentional act, a point Findlay also refers to. H. Plesser recalls how Husserl once told him that he had always sought reality and how Husserl in saying this gave graphic expression to both intentionality and its fulfilment by hitting his walking stick against the doorstep.

For Husserl intuition is not a 'receptivity to data' to which the intention adds a meaning. It is always dependent on, and functionally related to the intention (meaning). The intuition is the realization (*Erfüllung*) of the intention. To understand the meaning clearly thus would be the 'realization' of the intention. Intention and realization are, therefore, simply Husserl's terms for the beginning and of the process of clarification. Husserl believes that the task of the philosopher is to describe faithfully and honestly the things which are revealed in pure intuition. Description expresses what one has experienced. Philosophy thus is in terms of 'first person' experience. The practice of using first person experiences as the basis of philosophy goes back to Descartes, for whom *Cogito Ergo Sum* is the first philosophical truth. But after him, the interests of philosophers shifted to the third person experiences because they started looking for a common ground for communication. Also, thanks to the influence of the natural sciences and mathematics, philosophers became more interested in objectivity. In phenomenology first person experience once again became the source of all human knowledge.

The description of first person experience is vastly different from the description of the uses of languages by the analytical philosophers. The interest of the latter is not in personal experiences but in common language. They are on the whole rather critical of the whole idea of intuitive experience. Critics like Chappell says, "Both the phenomenologist's 'intuitive experience' and special objects supposedly revealed therein or by are, I believe, myths, and philosophically hampering myths . . .".[28] For Husserl, however, intuition has a wider connotation. It is much more than sensory perception. It is not mystical or psychological intuition. His view of experience is wide enough to include a large variety of intuitions. Intuition is "of a fundamentally unique and novel kind". It is not to be conceived as a lyric leap into the unknown, but rather a perfectly controlled process, which is self-justifying from beginning to end. It is not like a flash which is often to be found in traditional speculative metaphysics. Objects are not revealed in a flash of intuition but are received through a justified process. Husserl "posit(s) an intellectual intuition and thereby totally rationalizes his grasp of reality".[29] What Husserl tacitly insisted on in his use of 'Reason' in *Ideas,* is that the consciousness of objects is *both* the intuition of things themselves as well as the constitution of objects by Reason.

Husserl insists that philosophy should restrict itself to description of experience. He also insists that the result of this investigation will be essential truth and an unshakable foundation for all knowledge. For the rationalists reason only had the capacity to provide the universal and necessary elements in our experiences. What reason genuinely sees to be necessary, is necessary, in one way or another, this is the presupposition of all rationalism. For Husserl, however, necessity and universality is provided by pure intuition. All contingency is put aside by the epoche. Intuition in Husserl's phenomenology is an '*a priori* insight'. The objects of cognition are necessarily revealed through pure intuition. In other words, it is only in intuition that objects are revealed. For Husserl intuition is a "fundamentally rational operation because it . . . will be intentional through and through". The instrument of this thorough-going rationalisation of intuition is intentional constitution. What is given in intuition is evident because to be 'given' is to be constituted and to be apodictic is to be constituted rationally. Intuition shows the inevitability of the object in the act of experience. To say that the object is necessarily contained in the act of experience does not justify the meaning of an object. This is justified or fulfilled by immanent vision that Husserl called intuition.

What is the nature of the objects revealed in pure intuition? They are pure essences, general objects. Through the phenomenological reduction Husserl brackets out spatio-temporal objects and with the transcendental reduction objects are "located" 'in' the acts of experience. Description is now no more description of phenomena; it is description of a particular sort of phenomena, namely essences. In eidetic reduction particular objects are left behind in order to gain their essence. But essences, pure phenomena, are not a smoke-screen concealing the "thing in itself". On the contrary, what lies behind phenomena is no longer of interest. What is important is how they present themselves "immanently" in intuition. Husserl is concerned solely with how they appear and not with how they exist, still less with whether they exist. This attention to "what appears" terminologically implies a rejection of speculative metaphysics. Moreover, for Husserl physical reality, state of affairs, cannot be inferred from essences. Essences are fact-neutral. He treats facts and essences as two separate distinct worlds having no relation with one another. This arises from his rejection of the philosophical theory of "abstraction". From the essences "alone", Husserl explains, "we are not able to infer even the pettiest truth concerning the fact world".[30] This justifies J.N. Mohanty's statement that Husserl's phenomenology accepts "The principle of phenomenological discontinuity".[31] The facts and the essences are of different types which cannot be reduced to one another nor be inferred from one another. This sets a limit to all deductive metaphysics.

Husserl admits that while essences are presented to consciousness directly and non-inferentially, these presentations have varying degrees of clarity and exactness. Hence, he does not stop with the intuition of essences, but moves on to describe them in order to elucidate and increase their clarity. The "great task he (Husserl) envisions for phenomenology (is) the clarification, through description . . .".[32] He is aiming ultimately at the description of intuitive experiences. Now the problem of language in Husserl's philosophy arises especially in relation to this activity of description. The description of essences depends on the expression of intuition in a linguistic form. Language is to play a crucial role in re-presenting essences. It is also important that representation should acquire the unambiguous clarity that intuitive essences themselves possess. Language is, however, important because our experience is objectified and shared primarily through language. Language is the root of communication, and communicative systems cannot be bracketed out. This is why perhaps Husserl takes communication to be the original function of language. But a problem of expression always arises in intuitive philosophies, for intuition seems to be incompatible with communication. There is tension between the 'given' and the anticipated. The intuitive experiences are essentially individualistic and pre-predicative and their expression in language destroys their true character. But in spite of being handicapped language still plays an indispensable role in describing the essences.

Husserl's theory of language originates in his theory of meaning which has its original locus in the act of speaking. In *Formal and Transcendental Logic,* Husserl seems to be taking language as an original mode of disclosure of objects. Language springs from inter-subjective relations, and these struggle to articulate themselves through speech. Speech, in this way, has a concretizing function. Husserl concentrates on the living act of speaking. Language, consequently, consists in actual speaking and hearing, in living conversation. Speech is 'twofold', between speaker and hearer. Husserl's interest is not in the historical origin and growth of language, but in actual conversation. Language *per se* is not an objectified structure, but it is rather in the communicative situation that it becomes interesting for Husserl. Husserl writes "The environment *(Umwelt)* which constitutes itself in the experience of the other, in reciprocal understanding and in agreement, is called by us the *communicative* environment".[33] The objectivity of language is something which Husserl sees not so much in relation to and in contradiction to subjectivity as in relation to intersubjectivity. In this respect, "along with recent Anglo-Saxon philosophers, he sees the objectivity of language as something intimately involved with the concept of a 'common' world, and along with them, by implication at least, has grave doubt as to the possibility of a 'private' language".[34]

Like all other acts of experience, the experience of language is also noetic experience which produces an identity of word and content. Husserl says, while "speaking we are continuously performing an internal act of meaning, which fuses with the words, and as it were, animates them".[35] But a speech act, unlike other acts, have a certain universality. It is universal in the sense that of all other modes of consciousness, it permits the entire domain of consciousness to be 'mapped into itself'. Mute consciousness can be brought to speech, and as Mohanty says phenomenology as a science rests on this possibility.[36]

Like Wittgenstein, Husserl agrees that language is an activity. Although Husserl does not believe that the nature of linguistic activity can be correctly captured by the metaphors of playing games, he does assign a priority to speech acts over language as a system. The descriptive programmes of both Husserl and Wittgenstein depend on speech-acts. But how speech-acts are to be understood makes the difference. For linguistic analysts a speech act is a sort of rule-governed behaviour, whereas for Husserl a speech act is an intentional act which includes its sense as well as reference and is not a general lense through which everything is seen. Since speech acts of Husserl are intentional, meaning is constituted by an ideal correlation of noesis and noema.[37] "The primary locus of meaning is not the linguistic instrument, -- but rather the activity of an intentional consciousness".[38] Meanings are thus drawn into the activity of the ego which have been of significance from the very beginning in Husserl's philosophy. He emphasized the importance of the agent who performs acts in which meanings originate. Meanings are general objects. They cannot be "about" physical objects, for Husserl thinks 'the palm-trees' may prove to be a mirage. Meanings are beyond natural history. It was only in a much later development that Husserl attempted to connect such meanings with the factually given life world. While Husserl attempted to treat meaning somehow in terms of intentional relations, linguistic analysis conceived reference to objects as an indispensable factor in understanding the meanings of sentences. Analytical philosophers are very suspicious of the idea that meanings can be entertained in the mind in a pure state. They viewed meanings as a certain style of operation performed with words. But in phenomenology an operation involves a concentration, a fixing of attention . . . one recalls Husserl's use of the word "apperception" - containing the idea of a direction of the mind towards something beyond itself. Apperception is a specific activity of consciousness, it is a condition for identifying things in a number of different acts. Transcendental in immanence points to the activity of the ego. Meanings consist in the operation of the acts of consciousness, which are intended. Linguistic philosophers, on the other hand, are concerned with operations of linguistic rules. Their view is called operationalism. Here the stress is on "a style of operation" of using language.

Husserl, incidently, is not opposed to this operational approach but confines its validity to artificial languages, like that of arithmetic. He agrees that the meaning which the chess men possess in the game does not depend on the material of which they are made or the form which they have. It is found in the rules of the game which give them their meaning. But arithmetical signs also have a primitive meaning, which does not, however, enter into arithmetic for here their meaning is governed by the arithmetical operations in accordance with the established rules. Arithmetical signs are thus less ambiguous; their meaning is derived entirely from the "rules of the games". In Husserl's view an operational procedure of this kind has a limited validity. This is perhaps why Husserl adopts a more primitive meaning of signs and symbols, prior to their operational use – one could say a less technical meaning, more intuitive and natural. The Husserlian method makes logical operation dependent on meanings while the analytical philosophical method makes meanings depend on linguistic and logical operations.[39]

All operations of language, however logically formalized, originate somewhere else. This is to say that Husserl's doctrine of meaning, even though open to criticism, is an attempt to fill a gap which a purely operational definition leaves open. The intuitive grasp of meaning in Husserl's phenomenology has a certain edge over what the analytical linguistic philosophers say. A pre-verbal basis seems to lie behind the description of the various uses of language. But whereas Husserl's descriptive programme is based on intuition, it is, nevertheless, intuition itself which poses problem for his descriptive programme.

References

1. E. Husserl, *Ideas I,* p. 176.
2. *Ibid.,* p. 176.

3. *Ibid.*, p. 211.
4. *Ibid.*, p. 202.
5. *Ibid.*, p. 43
6. *Ibid.*, p. 178.
7. *Cf.* J.N. Mohanty, "Philosophical Description", *Philosophical Papers, First Series,* ed. by Kalidas Bhattacharyya, pp. 2-3.
8. E. Husserl, *The Idea of Phenomenology,* p. 10.
9. E. Husserl, *Ideas I,* p. 108.
10. *Ibid.*, p. 110.
11. E. Husserl, *Cartesian Meditations,* p. 151.
12. *Cf.* C.A. Van Peursen, "Edmund Husserl and Ludwig Wittgenstein", *Philosophy and Phenomenological Research,* 1959-60, Vol. 20, p. 183.
13. E. Husserl, *Cartesian Meditations,* p. 150.
14. H. Spiegelberg quotes Husserl, "Husserl's way into phenomenology for Americans : A letter and its sequal", *Phenomenology : Continuation and Criticises,* ed. by F. Kersten etc.
15. E. Husserl, *Cartesian Meditations,* p. 27.
16. E. Husserl, *The Idea of Phenomenology,* p. 37.
17. J.O. Urmson, *Philosophical Analysis,* p. VII.
18. *Cf.* E. Husserl, *Cartesian Meditations,* pp. 46-48.
19. E. Husserl, *Ideas I,* p. 182.
20. *Ibid.*, p. 121.
21. *Ibid.*, p. 242.
22. E. Husserl, *Logical Investigations,* Vol. I (2nd Edition) Eng. tr. p. 252.
23. E. Husserl, *Philosophy As Rigorous Science,* Eng. tr. by Quentin Lauer, pp. 96-97.
24. *Ibid.*, p. 146.
25. M. Heidegger, *Being and Time,* Eng. tr. by John Macquarrie etc. p. 58.
26. Husserl, *Ideas I,* p. 92.
27. Eiichi Shimomisse, quotes Husserl, "Philosophy and Phenomenological

Intuition", *Ana lecta Husserliana,* Vol. VIII, pp. 64-65.

28. V.C. Chappell, "Ego and Person: Phenomenology or Analysis", *Monist,* Vol. 49, 1965. p. 19.

29. Quentin Lauer, Introduction to English translation of *Phenomenology and the Crisis of Philosophy,* by Husserl, p. 43.

30. E. Husserl, *Ideas I,* p. 57.

31. *Cf.* J.N. Mohanty, "Individual Fact & Essence in Edmund Husserl's Philosophy", *Philosophy and Phenomenological Research,* 1959, Vol. 20, pp. 222-30.

32. Suzanne Cunninghum quotes Rebert Sokolowski, *Language and the Phenomenological Reductions of Edmund Husserl,* p. 40.

33. J.N. Mohanty quotes from Husserl's *Ideen* in *E. Husserl's Theory of Meaning,* p. 65.

34. Margaret Chatterjee, "Language as Phenomenon", *Philosophy and Phenomenological Research,* 1969, Vol. 30, p. 118.

35. E. Husserl, *Formal and Transcendental Logic,* p. 22.

36. *Cf.* J.N. Mohanty, Husserl's *Theory of Meaning.* Introduction to the Third Edition, p. xxiii.

37. *Cf.* Apel/Mohanty/Quinton "Discussion: Theories of Meaning in Analytical and Continental Traditions", *Graduate Faculty Philosophy Journal,* 1978, Vol. 7, pp. 79-105.

38. Maurice Natanson, "Phenomenology and the Natural attitude", *Literature, Philosophy and the Social Science,* p. 40.

39. *Cf.* C.A. Van Peursen, *Phenomenology and Analytical Philosophy,* pp. 92-96.

5

Limits of Description

HUSSERL'S philosophy as pointed out earlier is a philosophy of intuition. The essences are 'given' to pure intuition but in order to describe and analyse them, we have to use language. Their expression in language, however, involves a gap. Intuition is a clear vision but manifestation of this in language never do justice to all the fullness of such experiences. Language can never be a faithful expression of intuitive experience. To express intuitive experiences in language involves a leap from one level which is unmistakably different from that of speechless dealing with things *(Sache)*. By the very use of language and in bringing into being a universe of discourse we are unfaithful to our experience, by constantly substituting for it abstractions which disguise or betray it. Though language is not the only means of expression, it is yet a vital one. Without 'language' in the broadest sense of the term, the subject would be centered on itself and no genuine inter human relationship would be possible. Verbal expressions mediate between subjects, not despite but precisely because of their objective force. It is necessary to postulate a 'filter' for experience, which provides a 'filter of language' an element in virtue of which the data of experience assume certain meanings for the subjects.[1] Description is an explicit linguistic function, that which articulates the meaning of data. To say that an expression is 'filtered' is to say that it is capable of being described, no more no less. Description is simply the explication, the explicit version of the experiences in terms of that in which data assume meaning. Experiences are thus objectified in description. It seems that both intuition and its expression in language are essential for description, and yet that the expression of intuition in language does not always do justice to intuitive experiences.

There is inevitably a paradox of the situation of expression in Husserl's philosophy.[2] The paradox occurs when transcendental phenomenology makes itself known to the world. The phenomenologist must need speak the language of the natural attitude in order to be understood. Transcendental insights are thus poured into the mould of natural language. But since language always falls short of expressing experiences faithfully, phenomenologist encounters an internal contradiction between "mundane word-meanings and their transcendental sense".

There is also a similar gap in linguistic analytical philosophy between what is pointed out and what is said. What is pointed out is the general structure of the language and what is said illustrates the particular use of the language. The gap between universal and particular persists. The linguistic philosophers are interested not so much in the meaning of particular expressions as in the general structure of linguistic understanding. It is important to notice that the step from the analysis of word-meaning to the analysis of the structure of linguistic understanding is not just a step from the less to the more but from particular to general. The structure which is being analyzed, although linguistic, is not given in words at all. On the contrary philosophers have to invent new words (or new meaning for old words) in order to describe the structural aspects they are interested in (e.g. 'reference', 'illocutionary act' etc.,). It is generally conceded that language is mysterious. It is neither a thing nor a fact. It has an ambiguous status. This point made by the linguistic philosophers must be conceded. Not only phenomenologists and linguistic philosophers but all those who practised any kind of reductive method also switch from one level to another level. The reductive method purports to reduce one type of phenomena into another type of phenomena. This is done for the sake of clarity but it involves a jump nonetheless. The translation fron one level to another can never quite come off. However, reductionism involves abstraction either by pricing away elements from concrete facts or by symbolising concrete facts through formal devices. Such abstractions, however, deceive us with regard to the nature and meaning of concrete facts. An irony indeed.

For phenomenologists, especially for Husserl, the first condition for philosophising is to adopt a reflective attitude, Husserl asked us to leave behind the straightforward naive attitude and to adopt a critical, detached and reflective stand. In this way phenomenology signifies an attitude of thought, a specifically philosophical attitude of thought. It is a question of modifying the ordinary attitude which people assume towards their environment. It is in the theory of the everyday world rather in the praxis of the everyday world that Husserl's interest lies. Here *theoris* dominates and not *praxis*.

If for Husserl the task of philosophy is to reflect, this means he is advocating a certain kind of *activity*. He emphasizes the activity of "apperception" of consciousness. The characteristic of this activity is that it necessarily involves attending to the content of the experience. This emphsizes the implicit theory in the reflective activity. The phenomenological attitude is a theoretical rather than a practical one, but to be sure it involves its own kind of practice and method whose ultimate purpose is simply to 'see' or to 'know' which is in turn characterised in terms of "correct theoretical thinking". The act of experience is necessarily tied up with the content of the experience. So Husserl's method of critical reflection offers a threat to his descriptive programme in the following way. The reflective process necessarily embraces the object of experience. In the act of experience, a person 'looks' to the object which is contained in the experience. To reflect on experience is not simply to describe it but to go further and search its inherent structures on the noetic and noematic sides. The limits of reflection pose limits to description. Reflection becomes more and more complex as thought advances and leads eventually to a whole science, to a science of beginnings, a 'first' philosophy. All philosophical descriptions, the very foundation of all sciences whatsoever, spring from its matrix. Husserl's aim is to provide this 'First Philosophy' which shall be "valid once for all times."

But in spite of his claim to have pioneered a descriptive phenomenology, Husserl is not uninfluenced by the methodology of a philosophy of a very different kind, that of Descartes' rationalism. His *Cartesian Meditations,* after all, are a commentary on Descartes' method. The Cartesian ideal of making philosophy an exact science never left Husserl's mind. His search for 'ideal truths', 'truths in themselves', 'absolute certainty', for an unshakable foundation of human knowledge which he referred to as the 'Archimedean point', puts him squarely in the rationalistic philosophical tradition. It is of decisive and ultimate significance for Husserl's phenomenology to try to discover a begining that has no presuppositions and to undertake, as a methodological starting point, an "overthrow", not only of habitual prejudices but also of all existing sciences. In his idea of a rigorous science based on evidence and developed on the model of certainty, the impact of Descartes' mathematical rationalism is not difficult to trace. Cartesian redicalism is pre-eminently present in the very motto with which Husserl put forward for his programme, a radical reform of philosophy in the shape of a 'rigorous science'. But the rationalistic quest of certainty goes against the very idea of the descriptive programme. The concept of certainty is usually tied up with the formal sciences and if the descriptive programme has to be ventured on the quest of such a type of certainty it only proves to be an *ignis fatuus*. Although Husserl belongs quite definitely to the company of those who feel that absolute knowledge is attainable, yet he does not believe in *the* Absolute. Nor of course did Descartes.

As stated in the first chapter, descriptive philosophy arose as a reaction against speculative philosophical systems. Husserl's description is no exception to this. He criticised Hegel as the latter's conception of philosophy was tied up with his concept of system whereas for Husserl the demand that philosophy be 'scientific' was identical with the demand that it be systematic. Here the Kantian element in Husserl shows itself. But actually this is something that Husserl did not always adhere to. From statements in some of his letters and fragments now found in his unpublished manuscripts it appears that Husserl cherised something which he himself called a system. His aim "is to testify to a significant revolution in philosophy and to prepare the ground for the future philosophical 'systems'."[3] What Husserl had in mind, of course, was different from traditional philosophical systems. He never said that there is just *one* comprehensive, absolute system which could account for all phenomena. For him there are "noetic-noematic systems of essences which must permit of being systematically described and determined according to possibilities and necessities".[4] The 'systems' of Husserl are none other than regions of being. His philosophical system is neither speculative nor absolute; they can be revised and hence are not closed. But it is not, however, off the mark to say that Husserl's philosophy is not free from the charges of atomism. It believes that there are absolute simples out of which "the world" is to be "logically constructed". There are objects, independently of any linguistic context, that are epistemologically absolute data. The generic view that there are absolute rock bottom elements has been rejected by any descriptive philosophy.

Some maintain that the task of description of experience can be undertaken better by existentialists and that their approach is nearer to the descriptive programme than the transcendental phenomenology of Husserl has been found to be. They reintroduce existence and situate experience in a practical rather than in a theoretical context. The existentialists reject the idea of philosophy as an 'academic pursuit'. They are against 'interpretation without action' and that is why Sartre finally looked in the direction of Marxism. They are against academic theorizing with a strong anti-rationalist bias. Instead of "I think" they emphasize "I can", "I am able to do". In other words, man "materializes" his existence primarily not through theoretical knowledge but in concrete doing, acting and making i.e. in his "practical" concern with things and with his fellow men. The existentialists think that from our own immediate experience it can easily be shown that all meanings which are found in our theoretical knowledge refer back to a "primordial praxis" in which they originated. Moreover, the existentialists frankly recognise the influence of culture and history, the way in which the experiences of man are influenced by his environment. As for Husserl, with the suspension of the natural world, he bracketed out change also. He claims to be looking only for the essential structure of experiences which are time neutral. His transcendental philosophy is true for all times and is culture-free. The essences are non-temporal. Husserl said we must not sacrifice eternity to time. Thus while describing essences, Husserl left behind historicity. But he is certainly wrong here. The objects of description cannot be time neutral, they cannot be immune to history. Whether or not the charge of Platonism, against Husserl be correct (charge of Platonism applies to the *Prolegomena* and *First Logical Investigations)* he is certainly guilty of leaving out historicity. What is given in experience and how it is given, presupposes a *definite* temporal background and such a context is found to be a feature intrinsic to experience itself. Description of the acts of experience and objects of experiences necessarily includes reference to time, change and the social environment. This is why in the later years of his academic career, Husserl felt the need of writing *The Phenomenology of Internal Time-Consciousness.*

It could be maintained that the greatest threat to Husserl's descriptive philosophy arises from its subjectivity. Like Kant his philosophy is transcendental and in this lies both its merit and its limitation. His theory of knowledge, theory of meaning, theory of language, his attitude towards the world and also his descriptive method all are transcendentally oriented. The dichotomies Husserl tries to come to terms with in philosophy are not rationalism verses empiricism but objectivism (which includes both rationalism and empiricism) versus transcendentalism. Transcendental philosophy is above all the critique of objectivism and Husserl's last work *The Crisis of European Sciences and Transcendental Philosophy* is the best example of this. Philosophy is radically different from the natural sciences. This is the ground theme of this work. Husserl fought against objectivism till the last, finding a common ground for human communication in the lived experiences of life-worlds. For Wittgenstein also philosophy lies either 'above or below' the natural sciences but is never on the same level as it is. But while for Husserl philosophy is different from the sciences because the latter are essentially objective and the former is transcendental, for Wittgenstein, philosophy is different from science because philosophical statements are different from scientific statements. The statements of natural sciences are informative, they are true or false, but philosophical statements are truth-value neutral and are only elucidatory. They do not give any information, their function is only to clarify. The situation is a little tricky for Wittgenstein for he keeps philosophy away from the sciences and yet accepts objectivity, a main characteristic of the natural science. Philosophical statements, according to Wittgenstein are not subjective. They are not about private experiences. In fact Wittgenstein questions the very possibility of private language. Language games follow rules which are not personal. Language games are accepted practices in society. They have universality and objectivity. Gellner believes that this objectivism necessarily amounts to naturalism. Analytical philosophers are, in his view, guilty of naturalistic metaphysics and his criticism at this point seems to be valid.

A trap awaits for those who opt for description of language and also those who opt for description of pure experiences. Both parties distinguish philosophy from the natural sciences and logic and yet both are nevertheless strongly influenced by them. Husserl aimed at making philosophy a rigorous science. This is no doubt different from the natural sciences, but the aspiration for a scientific basis for philosophy is still very much in evidence. Since the time of Descartes there has been a widespread desire among philosophers to give philosophy the status of a science. Husserl and Russell, two prominent philosophers in recent times, are no exception to this.

For Husserl, however, philosophy as rigorous science is essentially transcendental. Transcendental philosophy for him is "the basic philosophical science, preparing on descriptive lines the transcendental ground which remains henceforth the exclusive ground for all philosophical knowledge".[5] Husserl tried to provide a transcendental basis for philosophical description. But can a genuinely transcendental philosophy be descriptive? The 'transcendental turn' requires a move from straightforward dealing with the world to a consideration of the world as meant and this is done by Husserl with the help of the transcendental reduction. A philosophy is transcendental if it is concerned not so much with objects as with our manner of knowing objects. No doubt Husserl's subsequent programme of descriptive study of phenomena in their essential structures was widely understood as a "turn to the objects" and turning away from the subject, and his main question became how is the world given? How are objects given? Yet the answer to this question is provided *a la* Kant in terms of subjectivity. Objects are revealed only in the acts of experiencing. The specific activity of consciousness, "apperception", is the condition for identifying things through a number of different acts. The object is constituted by the pure Ego.

Husserl's aim is no doubt to describe what is directly presented. Intentionality (the noesis and noema relation) takes on the constitutive and Kantian role of being that feature of our looking at the world thanks to which there is a world of objects for us to look at. Constitutive intentionality is creative in character. There is something dynamic in the way in which knower and known are inter-related. However, some of Husserl's commentators like Robert C. Solomon think that Husserl departs from the descriptive programme in adopting constitutive phenomenology. Descriptive phenomenology is in fact different from constitutive phenomenology. He argues that since intuition is different from constitution, descriptive philosophy which is essentially intuitive cannot be constitutive. He further argues that Husserl never succeeded in resolving this conflict between consciousness as a passive receptor of intuition and consciousness as an active constitutor of objects.[6] Thus the difference between description and constitution for him lies in the difference between the passive grasp of objects by intuition and the active constitution of objects by the pure Ego. This criticism, however, is not altogether valid. Husserl presents his philosophy in such a form as to combine both intuition and constitution. He strives hard to minimize the conflict (if there is any) between intuition and constitution. The noema which is given in intuition, is nevertheless, constituted by the acts of consciousness of which it is an object. Thus Husserl came very near to Kant's notion of the "synthetic unification of apperception by the understanding" in his doctrine of the 'given' in intuition except that the unifying factor for Husserl is not judgement as it was for Kant, but the intentional thrust of consciousness itself. Those who differentiate between description and constitution in Husserl's philosophy have in fact 'descriptive psychology' in mind. They differentiate descriptive psychology and not descriptive phenomenology from constitutive phenomenology.

In the preface to *Logical Investigations* Vol. II[7] Husserl identified phenomenology with "descriptive psychology" in spite of his earlier polemic against psychologism. It was in the essays on *Logical Investigations* that Husserl discussed the concept of intentionality for the first time. Following Brentano, he held that all mental acts are intentional. But at this stage in his thinking a true description of a mental act does not necessarily reveal the existence of the intentional object. The doctrine of intentionality recognises that all mental acts are, in principle, fallible. Later on, however, he left 'descriptive psychology' and introduced transcendental phenomenology. The concept of intentionality, consequently, underwent modification. Now every act of experience, according to Husserl, necessarily contains an object of experience, a content. The pure Ego constitutes the object in the act of experience. The unity of noema and noesis is directly presented in pure intuition and it is this that Husserl aims at describing. Descriptive phenomenology essentially involves constitution but 'descriptive psychology' does not.

The preceding discussion, may be taken to show that objects are dependent on the act of experience. Perhaps because of this some thinkers thought that Husserl's descriptive phenomenology must need involve transcendental idealism. In 1907 and in subsequent years Husserl came to the conclusion that the subjective pole of the relation between noesis and noema was the decisive one. Not only the critics, but Husserl himself accepted his phenomenology as transcendental philosophy[8] because of his insistence that all objects exist in virtue of their constitution by consciousness. The doctrine of the relativity of the world and the absoluteness of consciousness is at the heart of his idealism. He argues that if we give up this doctrine we fall back to naturalistic, dogmatic and uncritical philosophy. And anyone who falls back into this position surrenders the claim that philosophy is rigorous science. Thus, paradoxically, in order to uphold descriptive philosophy, idealism is conceded. Paul Ricoeur says "it is difficult to separate the description from the idealistic content".[9]

"Positing" has ever been a crucial activity for idealist. The world is "posited" by the mind. Despite his innovative techniques, Husserl's standpoint conforms in many ways to the traditional idealist stance. Being depends upon being known. All known reality is related to a knower. For Husserl all reality exists through our dispensing of meaning.[10] Marvin Farber says : "When Husserl forsakes his originally conceived methodological device for questioning all beliefs and proceeds to argue . . . that objects are only conceivable in a subjective context, he is no better off basically than Berkeley."[11] But certainly Husserl's transcendental idealism is different from the subjective idealism of Berkeley. Husserl argues that being for consciousness must be understood not in a psychological sense but in a transcendental way. In place of "bad subjectivity", "bad idealism", he calls for "transcendental idealism", it must be remembered as he insists that his standpoint does not involve denial of the real existence of the world. It only seeks to clarify the sense of the world, the very sense in which it counts for everyone as really existing. But his long struggle to achieve clarity in this area finally resulted in a solution more like transcendental idealism than anything else.

If the charge of idealism against Husserl is justified then his philosophy can hardly be deemed descriptive at the same time. Descriptive philosophy, historically, arose as a reaction against idealism. Moreover, not only realists criticised Husserl for his idealism but his own students criticised him for adopting the idealists' path. The inclusion of the pure Ego caused a considerable stir, particularly among the members of the phenomenological school, who regarded it as an regrettable lapse into metaphysics, "a staying away from their primrose path of descriptive philosophy". The pure Ego, thus, proved to be another big stumbling block to Husserl's descriptive programme. But the pure Ego actually is not a hindrance to his descriptive programme, for it is this factor which makes description possible. The agent is indispensable for the descriptive programme. Can there be description without a describer? The question always arises "whose experiences do the philosophers describe?" Like Kant, Husserl does come to terms with the question of the conditions of the possibility of description. This important aspect of descriptive philosophy is completely missed by the linguistic analytic philosophers. Description of the various uses of language simpliciter is a disjointed description of language. There is a need for some underlying factor which unites the various uses of language.

The pure Ego, in Husserl's philosophy, is the basis of description but "it is in and for itself indescribable; pure Ego and nothing further".[12] He considered the transcendental Ego as the first principle from which everything else gets meaning. The pure Ego is the centre of reference. The ultimate terminus of the act of experience is the 'pure I', the 'pure Ego'. In Husserl, as in Descartes and Kant, we find that every *Cogitatio* (thought) requires a *Cogito*. "The *'I think' must be able to accompany all my presentations*".[13] The Ego is unchangeable absolutely simple and empty of all content. It cannot be thought of as separated or distinct from its own life. Taken in and for itself, the pure Ego is the functional centre of the stream of experiences. The Ego is "permanently even necessarily there". It is the "referential centre", "functional centre", an "Archimedean point", a "centre of radiation", a "non-participant onlooker", and it is characterised as "phenomenological meditating Ego", "reflecting ego". It is the "polarity" of the Ego to which intuition "happens". Husserl thus concludes *"The thesis of my pure Ego . . . is necessary and plainly indubitable".*[14] The pure Ego is the terminus of all philosophical inquiry. It is from the Ego-pole that intentionality gets its meaning. The strength of Husserl's descriptive programme is his theory of the pure Ego. But how the logical structural subject is to be related to empirical man, to the natural "I", is a problem that Husserl is never quite able to surmount. The irony is transcendental philosophy seems to thematize the human being as the starting point of analysis only in order to immediately leave behind it as a concrete being.

Also, on other accounts Husserl's descriptive programme is not free from defects. His theory of knowledge, for example, pulls against the descriptive programme on account of his insistence on subjective conditions for knowledge. The noetic conditions of knowledge, for Husserl, are revealed in the inseparable relation between act of experience and content of experience. In his view knowledge is incorrectly understood both by realism and subjective idealism. There has been a constant oscillation between realism and idealism throughout centuries of the history of philosophy. But both of them have incomplete theories of knowledge. To Husserl all the basic errors of the theory of knowledge go hand in hand with 'metabasis'. The subjective idealists, for example Berkeley, mistook human psychology for consciousness. This leads to "psychologism" for it dissolves the world in subjective events.

Against subjective idealism stands realism which recognizes the subjective act of presentation of the world, but tries to build a bridge from consciousness to the world outside. This is brought about through causal reasoning.

Husserl thinks that the dualism of objects of knowledge and acts of knowledge is what is mainly responsible for the traditional problem of knowledge. Usually we believe that objects are determined "in themselves", and that the contribution of knowledge is to discover the determinations that exist "in themselves" and to establish them "objectively" as they are "in themselves". The idea of the world as something out there which is investigated through the exact methods of sciences is generelly regarded as self-evident. Even if the universal applicability or sole validity of the "exact" method of natural sciences is not recognised by certain philosophers, the style of this mode of knowledge is regarded as a model. Though epistemological dualism is as old as philosophy itself, Husserl traces its modern origin to the natural sciences whose decisive feature is mathematical. It is primarily to Galileo that Husserl traces the transformation of science of nature into a mathematical science. For Galileo, exact and inter-subjective valid knowledge of the real world can be attained by the method of treating everything about this world as an example of a geometrical object or relationship. The guiding principle for rationalist philosophers was that of arriving at knowledge about the real world which is comparable in exactness, universality and inter-subjective agreement to the knowledge obtained in pure mathematics. In adhering strictly to the transcendental approach Husserl, however, found in the objectivism of the natural sciences, a model which had dominated philosophers in modern era, his main target of criticism.

Knowledge, for Husserl, lies in a "wholly new dimension". Epistemological "investigations lie outside the domain of all objective science and in a certain sense of any science whatsoever".[15] From the transcendental phenomenological point of view the very supposition of a world "outside" us is incorrect. The central concept in Husserl's transcendental analysis of knowledge is that of an actual meaning-giving objectivity constituting subjectivity. Moreover, phenomenology concerns itself with the ideal factor in the process of knowledge particularly the activity of the "I". It analyzes the subject's contribution to knowledge. The "riddle" of our knowledge of the transcendent is solved by means of a description of the ways in which objects do not exist independently of the acts of experience, rather they are revealed in the very act of experience. Description of the inseparable relation between act of knowing and object of knowing is the basis of knowledge. Thanks to such a description, the claim of consciousness to "reach" an object is vindicated and is made free of all mystery. This discussion of the theory of knowledge, however, suggests that Husserl is providing a critique of knowledge. For linguistic analytical philosophers also, description of the uses of language amounts to a critique of knowledge. But whereas they are doing it at the conceptual level, Husserl's interest is in the transcendental aspect. The linguistic philosophers emphasize the objective side by investigating logical rules and linguistic structures. Husserl is interested in the subjective side. Knowledge for Wittgenstein is tied up with the correct use of language, and since the traditional philosophers, according to him, are guilty of misusing language they naturally give a wrong theory of knowledge.

Now if a programme is critical, whether Wittgensteinian or Husserlian, can it be descriptive? A critique provides for the reformation of philosophy. Description, on the other hand, is the humble task of expressing in language what one 'sees' or 'how it looks'. The function of description is to clarify and elucidate and not to reform. Herein lies a contradiction in both Husserl's and Wittgenstein's programme. From Husserl's standpoint, a transcendental critique of knowledge is part of a phenomenological theory of the world and can fulfil its task adequately only within the context of a transcendental ontology. Husserl's ultimate concern lies in elucidating the meaning of the world in terms of subjectivity. Husserlian phenomenology, in fact, contains two conflicting motives. It aims at being a descriptive science of essences and essential structures belonging to different regions and it also stands for an endless process of clarification of meanings which are constituted in the rich life of human consciousness. If the first motive is more original, the second one is more persisting.[16]

Husserl's philosophy is often criticised on the ground of involving subjectivism. But while Husserl's philosophy expresses subjectivity it is not subjectivistic. Subjectivism is a philosophical standpoint which is essentially individualistic and cannot be shared by others. Husserl's interpretation of subjectivity, while on the other hand, emphasizing the role of the subject in the formation of knowledge, affirms that such knowledge is sharable and can be communicated. Husserl brings in the concept of life-worlds in order to solve the problem of inter-subjectivity. Life worlds provide the objective context without landing us in Galilean objectivism. Husserl's concept of life-world was supposed to free us from both subjectivism and scientism. All human beings have one common matrix of communication. This is not the physical world but the world of living-experiences. Life-worlds are the fundamental contexts of inter-subjectivity within which the transcendental Ego constitute meanings. The transition from the natural world to *Lebenswelt* means the transition from language to speech, to interpersonal communication. The environment which constitutes itself in the experience of the other in reciprocal understanding and in agreement, is a communicative environment. Within this environment a person enters into relationships with other persons. The *I* is relative to the *we*.

It is out of this interpersonal situation that language as an objectified structure arises in Husserl's philosophy.[17] Husserl emphasized the immediate life-world of the individual with the ego at its centre, as distinguished from the uncentred, objective world of modern Galilean science. The life-world is a pre-scientific and pre-logical world. The world of everyday life is the *"forgotten sense foundation of physical science". Labenswelt* is concealed, it goes on without being noticed. It is this failure to notice the concealing activity of the structures of life-worlds which resulted in an "objectivism".[18] Husserl thinks that every scientific discovery has its meaning foundation in this immediate experience. The "world of life" is already rich in meaning before the scientist begins his work. Husserl finds the "pre-predicative experience of our life-world as the matrix of all our predicatives and scientific knowledge."[19] In the modern philosophical tradition, the life world was never considered "in its own right", because of the over-riding pre-occupation with science. The inclusion of the life-worlds in Husserl's philosophy is not only part of his critique of objectivism, but it presents a new critique of Kant's transcendental philosophy. From Husserl's standpoint Kant's transcendental turn did not begin at the right place, for before that turn could be properly accomplished the idea of the life world must be worked out.

Moreover, the notion of life-worlds provides the essential context which makes Husserl's descriptive programme philosophical, just as forms of life provide the essential basis for Wittgenstein's descriptive programme. Descriptive philosophy necessarily requires a framework, a context through which description is possible. The 'forms of life' and 'life-world' are the 'axis of reference', the ultimate sheet anchor of description in Wittgenstein and Husserl. For Husserl there is a wide and rich horizon in the form of the historical everyday life world. The horizon of the life-world arises at the same time as the awakening of consciousness.

Things lying beyond the horizon have no meaning for Husserl. All human praxis takes place within horizon of life-world and has significance within them. The life-world may be regarded as a horizon within which all other worlds are constituted and given. It is not itself another world. It is not only the horizon within which other worlds are there but is also the condition of their possibility, and is thus itself a most comprehensive *a priori.* Husserl further says that the life-world is not an entity, also the plural makes no sense when applied to it. It is a field, a framework, which is necessarily and constantly given. The life-world is the pre-predicative world, a "world of sense experience". In this way the world of immediate experiences is the original ground of all theoretical and practical activities. It is the essential horizon through which the world thesis receives its essential meaning. The life-world enables meanings, experiences and consciousness itself. It is life-world which enables "givenness" which is the basis of descriptive philosophy. The experienced *Lebenswelt* offers the content whose essential structure consciousness will uncover. Husserl places the notion of *Lebenswelt* in a central position from which consciousness can proceed to uncover the foundation which made that very experience itself possible. In other words, it is the life-world which makes the description of experiences meaningful. Husserl thinks that the world of our experience should not be simply taken for granted. Rather he traces it back to its already "sedimented" historicity, that is, a historicity in which the world first acquires meaning as a world existing "in itself". The study of the essentials of experiences involves going back to the world as pre-given. To "go back" to the world of experience is thus to return to the life-worlds in which we already live. In other words return to the *Lebenswelt* is a condition of transcendental accomplished phenomenology.

The transcendental phenomenology culminates in the foundational discovery of the *"Lebenswelt"* as the reservoir of the lived experiences and as the irreducible basis of all meaning conferring activities. The life-world as the *"Sinn-fundament"* clarifies the issue how it is possible, remaining within the temporal flux of one's own life to intend meanings which are over-individual and are the basis of communication, understanding and translation.

Life-world is not merely a world of nature, but an intrinsically cultural world. It deals with value objects such as paintings, houses, articles of use, even practical dealings and expectation or in other words, the world of praxis, beauty, values, grief, care, and so forth as a world that derives meaning from communicative experience. Theoretical reason becomes practical reason, which then, however, is more closely connected with life, that is, with the life history of society then it is in the case of Kant "Reason" thus becomes a designation of an historical language, a call to overcome intellectual fatigue and to integrate all scientific reflection at the transcendental level.

Clarification of meaning requires us to return to those acts in which such a meaning could be intended. Husserlian phenomenology is a search for clarification of the meaning of the world in original *(ursprünglich)* experiences by tracing the genesis of higher order meanings back to the most fundamental layer of life-worlds. The life-world thus is "meaning fundamental". The theory of language in Husserl's philosophy also finds its place and justification through life-worlds. This immediate world is, however, self-constituting and precedes any description of it. It is the basis of descriptive philosophy. The life-world comes before any sense of objectivity arises; it is the 'pre-given' world. The life-world is never a given totality but rather always a presupposed "presumptive" totality. The life world notion for Husserl can be regarded as a 'limit' in a new sense, an enabling source to which we return again and again. It is out of this source that all possibilities of new description spring.

If the essential version of the Husserlian phenome-nology is nearer to the classical idealistic and rationalistic tradition, its concern with meaning brings it closer to the empiricistic tradition. There is certainly a 'tension' in Husserl's philosophy. There are two mutually antagonistic positions to which Husserl inclines. Firstly, a foundational one that inclines towards idealism, that there are ideal transcendental structures normative for all possible worlds and all human subjectivity and secondly, a historical one that inclines towards realism, that phenomena as "given" by the world are elicited by a historical culture, that they are never fully determinate, that they do not "mirror" the world as this is in itself, and that they are not composed of elementary, primitive parts "given" in a (culturally) non-relative way.

References

1. *Cf.* Philip Pettit, "On Phenomonology as Methodology of Philosophy", *Linguistic Analysis and Phenomenology,* ed. by Mays & Brown. pp. 245-46.
2. *Cf.* Kasuhis Misuno, "The Paradox of the Philosophical Method", *The Analecta Husserlians,* Vol VIII, pp. 37-51.
3. E. Husserls, *Philosophy As Rigorous Science,* Eng. tr. by Q. Lauer, p. 75.
4. E. Husserl, *Ideas I,* p. 376.
5. *Ibid.*, p. 15.
6. *Cf.* Robert C. Solomon, *From Rationalism to Existentialism,* p. 160.
7. *Cf.* E. Husserl, *Logical Investigations,* Volume II (First Edition).
8. *Cf.* E. Husserl, *Certesian Meditations,* p. 86.
9. Paul Ricoeur, *Husserl: An Analysis of His Phenonmenology,* p. 11.

10. *Cf.* E. Husserl, *Ideas I,* pp. 168-69.
11. Marvin Farber, *Phenomenology and Existence,* p. 24.
12. E. Husserl, *Ideas I,* p. 233.
13. Husserl quotes Kant, *Ideas I,* p. 173.
14. *Ibid.,* p. 145.
15. Husserl quoted by Iso Kern, "The Three ways to the transcendental Phenomenological reduction," *Husserl : Expositions and Appraisals,* ed. by Frederick A. Elliston etc., p. 139.
16. Mohanty, J.N., *The Possibility of Transcendental Philosophy,* p. 191.
17. *Cf.* J.N. Mohanty, *Edmund Husserl's Theory of Meaning,* (Third Edition), p. 65.
18. *Cf.* E. Husserl, *The Crisis of European Sciences and Transcendental Phenomenology,* pp. 68-70.
19. H. Spiegelberg, "Towards a Phenomenology of Experience", *Doing Phenomenology,* by H. Spiegelberg, p. 177.

6

Hazards of Philosophical Description

THE preceding chapters show that Wittgenstein and Husserl were doing different types of description and in different fields. The linguistic analytic philosophers practise conceptual analysis because for them philosophy is concerned with concepts. The phenomenologists, on the other hand, are concerned with the analysis of what they call "pure experience".

The stress on conceptual analysis made by linguistic analysts, however, suggests that they are inclined towards rationalism rather than towards empiricism. It is usually taken for granted that linguistic analysis is a later development of empiricism. And yet their emphasis on discourse indicates a certain bias towards rationalism. This, however, does not suggest that linguistic philosophers are doing what Descartes and other rationalists were doing. Linguistic philosophy deals with concepts no doubt, but it is not concerned with self-evidence as Descartes was. The linguistic analytic philosophical method, moreover, does not utilise any *a priori* device. Language is 'given' in natural communication. It has objectivity, it is something impersonal. The linguistic thinkers are not interested in how a word is used in a particular language but how it is used in all languages. This means that they are concerned with the conceptual aspect of a word.[1] Knowing the meaning of a word means knowing how to employ a concept. Concept terminology enables them to shift from the level of fact. Hence they talk of word meaning without doing linguistics. For linguistic philosophy functions in a conceptual framework of its own. The employment of concepts becomes intelligible not as a mental manipulation of more or less shadowy "ideas", but as the primary capacity for using words. This is what the later Wittgenstein thought about 'concepts'. The word 'concept' acquires a special meaning in his philosophy. The older philosophical literature on concepts was largely coincident with the treatment of universals. Analytical philosophers, however, are interested not in this so much as in linguistic behaviour at a high level of generality.

The phenomenologists, on the other hand, are concerned with the analysis of pure experience. A phenomenological description deals with what is given in experience, with experiences just as they show themselves. The aim is to bring to explicit consciousness the essence of what is experienced. Direct observation is the primary concern of phenomenology, and direct observation is held to be prior to all theory. In Husserl it is not discourse but 'seeing' which is important. The programme of "bringing essences to givenness", depends not on describing but on seeing.[2] That which is 'seen' cannot be explained away. It is the final court of appeal for all truly philosophical thought. Husserl's famous slogan "Back to the things themselves" emphasizes the aim of dealing only with what is given in direct experience. Husserl's interest is in "self-givenness" in experience. He regards *seeing* as final. All questions come to an end at this point. A thinker must "see" step by step. And it is an unwarranted demand to ask for a foundation or proof of "seeing" for this is the final terminus in philosophising. Husserl is interested in examining the intentional (meaningful, referential) experiences in order to determine what they may reveal or contain in terms of content. So in spite of the fact that Husserl is often dubbed an idealist or a

Platonist, and sometimes even said to be some sort of crypto-Cartesian, he is in fact an empiricist of a new kind. He does not deal with sense experiences as Locke and Hume do. Husserl's philosophy is a new and radical empiricism. For him nothing less than the full richness and complexity of experience can suffice as the scene of philosophical activity. He deals with all *kinds* of experience extending the term to all "conscious acts" in order to make room for what goes on in mathematical and logical thinking.

Moreover, for Husserl experience is always far *more* than what can be described in language. Experiences have a wider reach than language has. Language cannot capture in its nets all our experiences. The linguistic philosophers, of course, insist that every experience is 'filtered' through language. But are there not many experiences which cannot be put into language? The phenomenological treatment of experience goes deeper and realises the complexity and richness of human experiences. Indian philosophers also say language is not capable of expressing all human experiences. Novelists and poets also think that language always falls short of capturing total human experiences. Human experiences are the 'promised land' which cannot be totally accommodated within the framework of language.

But recognition of the unfulfilled potencies of experience leads not so much to a problem of description as to the idea of "what is witnessed to". The verbalisation of this witnessing will always be incomplete. The description of pure seeing is an "ideal" procedure and numerous difficulties of expression stand in its way. Since language falls short of expressing pure 'seeing', Husserl's pure descriptive programme remains programmatic.

While taking description into consideration both linguistic philosophers and phenomenologists seem to concentrate just on one aspect of it. It is almost as if the old co' ict between rationalists and empiricists had come up in a new form. Rationalism stressed linear thinking and empiricism stressed observation. Wittgenstein emphasized the importance of discourse, Husserl stressed "seeing". Being one sided their philosophies are subject to certain limitations. We are not here concerned with criticism of descriptive philosophy but rather with the hazards which inevitably arise in the way of faithful description and with the very idea of faithful description. Looking at these difficulties it may be asked whether the ritual of doing description in philosophy may not be too difficult to perform. However, instead of taking sides with respect to discourse, which is the sphere of the linguistic philosophers, and 'seeing' which is Husserl's main concern, the better thing may be to reflect on the conditions of description. Description does not strictly fall between discourse and intuition but may be to involve both of them. Kant's conditions of experience are in fact condition of description. Another attempt is made by Peter Zinkernagel in his *Conditions for Description.*[3] But Zinkernagel is concerned only with the conditions of scientific description and not with the conditions of philosophical description.

Philosophical description, whether phenomenological or linguistic, is tied up with the notion of analysis. Both analysis and description utilize piecemeal lucidation. The aim of every kind of philosophical analysis including the aim of Wittgenstein's and Husserl's descriptive programme is to clarify. And yet analysis and description do not seem to be quite compatible. The aim of the descriptive philosophy of Wittgenstein and Husserl is to describe what is 'given', without destorting its actual nature. Philosophical analysis of any type, on the other hand, has a commentatory aspect, often a reformative character and even an evaluative dimension. The aim of the philosophical analysis of an expression is not only clarifying how it is used, but also clarifying how best it can be used. If the analyst does not show that his way of arguing is the best among others, his analysis ceases to be philosophically effective. It degenerates into simply stating an opinion. Wittgenstein's and Husserl's descriptive programmes, however, are not so ambitious. They claim neither to establish theories nor to defend them.

Another consideration is that analysis can be informative. But philosophical description is non-informative and non-explanatory. In fact description in philosophy originated as a reaction to explanation. Wittgenstein always eliminated explanations from philosophy. In the *Zettel* he burst out "Why don't we just leave explaining alone?[4] Explanation is the forte of the natural sciences. Its use in philosophy only generates problems and confusions. The purpose of explanation, although carried on at the phenomenal level, is yet to dig out what is hidden, while philosophical description concerns only with what is 'given', i.e., what is "lying before us". Husserl no less than Wittgenstein criticised the use of explanation in philosophy. For him, explanation deals with the objective world, that is, with the world of the natural sciences, for scientists are concerned only with the causal explanation of phenomena. The method of philosophy by contrast is descriptive. But Marvin Farber argues that description cannot totally weed out all explanation. "Description is the ideal procedure, but it cannot always be achieved. Explanatory devices must also be used, and there are other types of reasoning and inquiry which are not descriptive in character."[5] This, however, is true only for scientific description because it is dealing primarily with causal matters. Causal chains are discovered by the sciences. It seems Farber must have been referring to deduction here when he speaks of "other types of reasoning". But since the descriptive method of both Wittgenstein and Husserl is essentially non-deductive, this particular part of Farber's criticism does not seem to apply to them.

Philosophy, for both Wittgenstein and Husserl, is different from the sciences. It is neither a formal nor a natural science. For Husserl philosophy is different from the sciences because the latter are essentially naturalistic while the former is transcendental, but for Wittgenstein philosophy is different from the science because philosophical statements are different from scientific statements. The natural sciences for both Wittgenstein and Husserl and, indeed, for anyone, are informative. Their aim is to provide knowledge, whereas the task for a philosopher, according to Wittgenstein and Husserl, is not to provide knowledge but to provide something else. One of the considerations which differentiates philosophy from the sciences is that the latter are essentially theoretical in nature whereas philosophy for Wittgenstein and Husserl is an activity, an activity of clarification. Descriptive philosophy for both of them moves from the theoretical to the practical in that both arrive ultimately to forms of life, life worlds where what we say finds its matrix. But to say this is actually to grant that the descriptive philosophy of both Wittgenstein and Husserl is neither theory-free nor culture-free. Both Wittgenstein and Husserl have as their programme the idea of reforming philosophy. Husserl sees radical reform of philosophy in the shape of a rigorous science. Wittgenstein wanted to reform the language philosophers use, to curb their pretensions. In doing this he was finally led to the consideration of the structure of language.

Wittgenstein's and Husserl's expositions always come in sequence,in order. Wittgenstein clearly says in *Remarks on the Foundations of Mathematics,* "I introduce order" in philosophy.[6] In his earlier work he was looking for an *a priori* order in the world. However, later on he talked about various orders in language instead of one fixed order. In *Philosophical Investigations* he says "We want to establish . . . many possible orders".[7] Not only Wittgenstein or Husserl but ancient philosophers also were primarily interested in the problem of order. The system builders believed in only one comprehensive order in the universe. Their primary aim was to discover the order of the real, for ancient philosophers were interested in *ontology* rather than in *meaning*. The characteristic of Wittgenstein's later work and Husserl's philosophy is that instead of speaking of one changeless order in the world, they talk about 'many-dimensional orders' to use Wittgenstein's phrase. So, as against the classical philosophers 'order monism' they introduced 'order pluralism'.[8] There are many ways the helper can be told to bring the mason 'slab, column, brick' in succession. There are unlimited ways in which words can function or sentences can be framed. Sentences do not have just one order. For Husserl an object does not appear in just one way but in many ways. There is a "dynamic framework of noetic-noematic correlativity", and instead of just one Absolute System, there are various systems of noetic-noematic correlation.

The primary task of the classical philosophers was of ultimate reality. They claimed to have given a complete view of the world, i.e., one which is true for everybody and true for all time. But both Wittgenstein and Husserl depart from classical world-views. They aim at a descriptive programme. And yet they both, in the last analysis, abandon description. The ultimate court of appeal is the forms of life and life-worlds. The piecemeal strategies with which they started are eventually swallowed up not in speculation but in the matrix which gave them birth. The matrix of the life-world and form of life is invoked in their descriptive programmes. In a sense this matrix, as we saw earlier, provides the limits for description. They both introduce the idea of "life" for the interpretation of phenomena. Meanings can no longer be separated in any respect from the field of the life-world, nor living language be reduced to the language of logical use. Every description and interpretation is rooted in the pre-theoretical *ordo amorous*.

Forms of life are the ultimate point of reference in Wittgenstein and the life-worlds are the index of reality in

Husserl. In the *Crisis* Husserl himself admitted the "Ontology of the *Lebenswelt*". While for both phenomenologists and existentialists there is often a technical distinction made between metaphysics and ontology, it is not too wide of the mark to say that the phenomenological movement became the source of a new world-view while at the same time offering a most serious critique of the metaphysical tradition. But instead of one comprehensive life-world, Husserl talks about various life-worlds and Wittgenstein talks about many forms of life. A common characteristic of both analytical philosophers and phenomenologists is that instead of advocating one world-view, they recognise the presence of many world-views. Russell also once said that the task of the philosophers was to provide many world-views.[9] Instead of speaking of *the* world the emphasis is on 'worlds'. There are various life-worlds and more new life worlds keep coming into existence. Also the interaction of various life-worlds gives rise to new forms of life. The philosopher is presented with an ever expanding field.

The concept of one comprehensive life-world belongs to dogmatic philosophy. For Husserl each individual has his own life-world. Life-worlds are also influenced by the 'historic-cultural frame of reality'. In this way life worlds are relative to culture and to personal history. Every subject has an original field of pure experience which is opened to him through free activity. The life world is "the pure field of original experiences" and since each of us has his own experience, "each of us has his own life-world". Without me the world, of course, means nothing to me. But I am not the creator of the world. I just experience it from my view-point. Every life-world has its horizon and history. Life-worlds are culturally relative. The life-worlds of mythico-magical societies are different from those of a modern society. The Chinese, Indian or European worlds are different from each other because the lived experiences that belong to them are of different types. They represent different cultures. Life-worlds differ from society-to-society, culture-to-culture. Husserl thus envisaged diverse life-worlds dynamically inter-related. They are by no means static, beyond all changes and modifications. Even though life-world has a relativity, it shows an invariant structure to which the relative and variable belongs. The life-world mainfests itself extended in space. It is the lived space and time.

The 'multi-levelled character' of life-worlds leads to multi-views of the world.[10] Each life-world is based on the individual's lived experiences. The traditional philosophy on such a view was too abstract and too remote from the field of our lived experience. It provided closed systems of reality. Life-worlds, however, are open-ended. They are moving, 'fluid', dynamic. They have numberless "offshoots" and have endless horizons. The concept of dynamic life worlds instead of a single absolute reality, provides the phenomenologist with a new key for solving philosophical problems.

Husserl had been critical of Dilthey's *Weltanschauungslehre,* on account of their (as he saw it) relativism. In Husserl's own case, although life-worlds are relative to individuals, this does not lead to relativism. Each life-world for Husserl is absolute in itself. Husserl does not speak about the Absolute World but for him each life-world is absolute in the sense that it is what it is. It needs nothing else to validate it. Each life-world has its own structure. Moreover, no question arises of adjudicating which life-world is true or false. Questions of truth and falsity were raised in classical philosophy. But the important thing for Husserl is that every life world is valid for itself.

Turning to Wittgenstein we find him stressing the various uses of words. This indicates that words too have various horizons for, according to Wittgenstein, we identify things through language and language is used in various ways. We identify things in multiple ways. Wittgenstein says, "To imagine a language means to imagine a form of life". Society influences language. It is not incorrect to say that since different societies have different languages they have different world-views. New uses of words can give rise to new world-views. Language, for Wittgenstein, is never fixed. New language games come into existence and others become obsolete and are forgotten.[11] Sense-datum language, for example, was at one time a new language game. In *On Certainty* Wittgenstein says "a language-game does change with time".[12] With the new language game, a new world-view originates. Gellner, who is otherwise a stern critic of linguistic philosophy, appreciated Wittgenstein's 'polymorphism' of linguistic usage. The description of the various uses of language freed Wittgenstein from the temptation to seek a "reduction" of one kind of experience to another.[13]

Here it may be pointed out that linguistic philosophy often considers the theory of world-views to be erroneous. It claims to be natural with regard to all substantive questions about the world. In fact, however, it does present an interesting, indeed striking, view of the world, which can be elicited from its discussion of criteria and from certain key sayings and occasional confessions. Moreover, it is interesting to see that Wittgenstein's acceptance of many forms of life is not all that different from *Weltanschauungslehre a la* Dilthey. For Dilthey all reflections on life are the product of particular individuals living at a particular time in a particular place determined by circumstances, influenced by the opinions around them, and bound by the horizons of their age. He grants that all such reflections are tinged with relativity. In spite of Dilthey's resolve to be true to experience and in spite of his recognition of its irreducible variety, he thought all our discussions of individual cases referred back to a comprehensive vision of reality. How can the philosopher who confronting the almost infinite diversity of life perceive any meaning or pattern in it? Dilthey replied that life is not a mass of disconnected facts. A philosopher uses certain principles for the organisation of his experience and so makes them meaningful. Dilthey called them categories of life. A particular experience in life has meaning in the framework of something non-relative. Wittgenstein, of course, does not speak about the categories of life but of a framework of everyday certainty. It is the metaphysics of everyday which underlies the innumerable forms of life. In this respect the world-view Wittgenstein himself adopts is nothing but naturalism. And here, of course, he is very different from Husserl.

The world-views which Wittgenstein and Husserl provide, however, paradoxically give an impression that they are at one step away remove from 'the natural world'. Both transcendental philosophizing and linguistic analysis are at one remove from the facts. Phenomenologists and linguistic philosophers maintain a 'distance' from the empirical world. Husserl started by bracketing out the empirical world. He was interested in the essential structures of pure experience and its world, and this is nothing but the *Lebenswelt.* Linguistic philosophers, however, hold contradictory views. On the one hand, they uphold naturalistic metaphysics and on the other, they talk about conceptual analysis which is certainly distinct from the empirical level. The conceptual level is always contrasted with the empirical level although it may ultimately refer back to it. This 'distance' is also to be found in the very expression of experience in language. To point out and express experience in language involves a gap. A question may be asked whether this 'distance' is inevitable. Is it necessary for descriptive philosophy to keep a 'distance' from the natural world? Descriptive philosophy started by recognising only the ordinary world and yet its procedure is such that, especially in Husserl's philosophy, it leaves the natural world behind. Such a tension seems to be inevitable in such philosophising.

In spite of the fact that the world-views presented by the descriptive philosophies of Wittgenstein and Husserl are open to criticism, it is interesting to note that the task of the philosopher for them, as for philosophers in the classical manner, culminates in some kind of world-views after all. If a philosopher does not provide an overall "standpoint", his procedure will resemble that of working scientists, that is, those who are interested primarily in piecemeal investigations rather than in general theory. But both Wittgenstein and Husserl make a big thing of differentiating philosophy from science.

Is there an alternative to the explanations which are found in science and the descriptions which are founded in world-views? The philosopher may make maps or use pictures in order to make his way in reality as is put forward in Ryle's *Dilemmas* or in Wittgenstein's phrase 'seeing as'. However, even here philosophers have a certain orientation of their own, each with his own method of expression. Reality thereby becomes symbolised. Doing this is neither to explain nor to describe but "to manifest" through maps and pictures, there is one more alternative to description and explanation, that is 'talk about talk'.[14] But 'talk about talk' has meaning only with reference to some overall view of the world. Ayer himself admits that it is indispenable to "examine the features of our conceptual systems" in order to "talk about talk". Concern with reality still lingers on amidst all these alternatives.

The characteristic of the world-views presented by Husserl and Wittgenstein is that they claim to set a man free. To be free is to invent a new world (for Husserl) or to put words to new uses (for Wittgenstein). For Husserl man has the capacity to make his own world. Husserl speaks of the "special motivation" which first of all frees man from his bondage to the world and to himself. All knowledge, all opinion, all belief regarding the world of things and human beings, stems from man's own experiences. Since life-worlds and forms of life are not fixed but dynamic, so also is man who is at the centre of them. Man is not here determined by his biological or physical constitution but is self-forming in the light of the cultural values he himself creates. In Husserl since the ego transcends the world of spatio-temporal existence, it is this which is the foundation of his freedom. In Wittgenstein's philosophy, man does not seem to be as free as he appears in Husserl's philosophy in that he is not absolutely free to use words as he likes, the use of words being related to natural human history and yet as society changes the use of words also changes accordingly. Human beings nevertheless are free to use new words for new situations. According to Waismann, man does not force his interlocutor. He leaves him free to choose, accept or reject any way of using his words. He may even use an expression at one time in this, and another time in that way. For Waismann "logic *constrains* us while philosophy leaves us free".[15]

The data of description changes with time, place and culture. The description of experiences and locations can never be the same for all time. The point is perhaps clearly seen by P.F. Strawson, "the task of descriptive metaphysics . . . has constantly to be done over again".[16] The results of descriptive philosophy are not assumed once for all in the sense in which the results of formal deductions can be absorbed in the development of logic or mathematics. Description involves a continual return to things themselves. Phenomenology is philosophy of experience, and to appeal to experience means to appeal to something *dynamic,* changing, shifting. The description of experience, therefore, cannot be fixed. Description even outside philosophy also does not always refer to static data. Scientific description changes with new discoveries in the sciences. Ordinary description (i.e. everyday description) as, for example, a cricket commentary which is surely a description of live play, is not static. But what differentiates a philosophical description from a non-philosophical one is that whereas the former cannot help being rooted in a metaphysical foundation, the latter does not require such a basis. It is forms of life and life-worlds which provide such a foundation. Without this, grounding descriptions would be anything but philosophical. Life-worlds and forms of life are introduced as the matrix out of which descriptive philosophy has its origin. The forms of life and life-worlds are appealed as the soil and of which experiences grow, something which is immune from either the justifying or the eroding work of argument.

Both Wittgenstein and Husserl felt that there is a bedrock which cannot be explained. The life-worlds and forms of life are precisely this in their philosophy. Now since life-worlds and forms of life are not free of categorical and cultural frameworks, this could lead us to "philosophical anthropology". Thinkers practising philosophical description say that nothing new is given by descriptive philosophy. But their philosophy in fact inevitably leads to philosophical anthropology. Anthropology emphasizes the multi-formity rather than the uniformity of human phenomena. Although Husserl remained suspicious of all on the anthropologies as further forms of psychologism, warning against it specifically in his lecture on "Phenomenological Anthropology",[17] even so there are anthropological frames of reference in his own discussion of worlds of experience. The reference to anthropology does not necessarily mean a capitulation to the objectivism which Husserl wanted to leave behind and the scientism which Wittgenstein also found it impossible for philosophy to emulate, but it witnesses simply to the acceptance of the history of multiple cultures.

Philosophical anthropology does not try to provide a science of human nature nor is it purely concerned with the history of society. It sets its sights rather on the manifold structures of human experience. Husserl's and Wittgenstein's philosophies are essentially *Lebensphilosophie* and as Pappé has commented to practise a *Lebensphilosophie* means to practise philosophical anthropology.[18] Wittgenstein had something to say about the role of primitive society in the development of human language and Husserl referred to the diversity of the life of societies, Chinese, Indian, European etc. Not only Husserl and Wittgenstein, but Locke and Hume also could be called philosophical anthropologists in that they were primarily concerned with the range of human faculties. Since their time, the traditional question "What is nature" has become the preserve of the natural sciences and philosophers' interest has shifted to man and his faculties.

Looking at all these consequences which necessarily follow from the descriptive philosophies of Wittgenstein and Husserl it may be asked whether, if the task of description is too difficult for philosophy to perform, what could be an alternative to it. In both linguistic analytic philosophy as well as in phenomenology, there are philosophers who have opted for other alternatives for they think that description as such is an ideal procedure and cannot always be performed. Most analytical philosophers, instead of describing philosophical statements, were interested in *classifying* them into different categories. Logical positivists, ordinary language philosophers and phenomenalists, were all concerned with questions of demarcation. Philosophical statements were divided into analytical and synthetic, *a priori* and *posteriori,* meaningful and meaningless, performative and non-performative, informative and non-informative. The interest of analytical philosophers is primarily in philosophical statements though not necessarily in their descriptive aspect.

Parallel to the analysts' interest in classification we have phenomenologists' interest in 'regions' of being. Among the existentialists Heidegger practised hermeneutic phenomonology. For Heidegger phenomena are not fully 'given' in pure intuition. They are hidden and in order to be meaningful the phenomena need to be 'interpreted'. Language helps in revealing the hidden phenomena. Language in Heidegger's understanding is quasi-magical. But language is magical because for him language is not simply one tool which man possesses along with many others; it is only language that makes possible our standing within openness to "what is". In its true origin language is poetry, and poetry is "the primal language of an historical people" in which it "found Being". Language is conceived as the house of Being. The function of language is not to describe what is directly 'seen' but to help in interpreting the hidden phenomena. For Marcel also unaided intuition is not an adequate philosophical instrument. He and Buber highlighted the revelatory and creative character of language rather than its descriptive function.

In these various ways the descriptive programme seems to give way today to a number of alternative strategies. Among these are the stress on categorical frameworks, a strategy which clearly leads from Kant to Poincare and which is perhaps scientific rather than philosophical; a philosophical anthropology which would take philosophy from the study to the market place; or a hermeneutic (existential or otherwise) which would no doubt have to recognise the conditioning factors at work on the philosopher himself. The descriptive programme in its two main forms which are discussed in this study with regard to Wittgenstein and Husserl performed an important function in weaning philosophers away from the vain attempt to emulate either the formal sciences or the natural sciences. But the idea of pure description is fraught with hazards. All experiences present themselves in the guise of *Ideenkleid.* Language here no doubt plays a key role, but language in its turn comes from a matrix which is non-verbal. Both Wittgenstein and Husserl are justly regarded as original thinkers of our times in no small part in virtue of their profound recognition of this fact.

References

1. *Cf.* A. Flew, "Philosophy and Language", *Essays in Conceptual Analysis,* ed. by A. Flew, p. 7.
2. E. Husserl, *Philosophy as Rigorous Science,* Eng. tr. by Q. Lauer p. 93.
3. Peter Zinkernagel, *Conditions for Description,* 1962.
4. L. Wittgenstein, *Zettel,* para 614.
5. M. Farber, *Philosophy and Existence,* p. 37.
6. L. Wittgenstein, *Remarks on the Foundations of Mathematics,* para 84.
7. L. Wittgenstein, *Philosophical Investigations,* para 132.
8. *Cf.* Paul Grimley Kuntz, "Order in Language, Phenomena and Reality : Notes on Linguistic Analysis, Phenomenology, And Metaphysics," *Monist* Vol. 49, 1965, p. 133.
9. *Cf.* B. Russell, *Our Knowledge of the External World,* pp. 72-73.
10. *Cf.* Robert D. Sweeney, "Affectivity and the Life World", *Analecta Husserliana,* Vol. V, p. 72.
11. *Cf.* L. Wittgenstein, *Philosiphical Investigations,* para 23.
12. L. Wittgenstein, *On Certainty,* para 256.
13. *Cf.* E. Gellner, *Words and Things,* p. 155 and p. 172.
14. *Cf.* A.J. Ayer, *The Concept of a Person,* p. 3.
15. F. Waismann, "How I see Philosophy", in *How I see Philosophy,* ed. by R. Harre, p. 21.
16. P.F. Strawson, *Individuals,* p. 10.
17. E. Husserl, "Phenomenology and Anthropology", *Philosophy and Phenomenological Research,* Vol. II, 1941 pp. 1-14, Eng tr. by Richard Schmit reprinted in *Phenomenology and the Background of Realism,* ed. by R.N. Chisholm.
18. *Cf.* H.O. Pappé "Philosophical Anthropology", *Encyclopaedia of Philosophy,* ed. by Paul Edward, Vol. 6, p. 169.

Bibliography

Alston, William P. "Philosphical Analysis and Structual Linguistic", *Journal of Philosophy,* Vol. 59, 1962, pp. 709-20.

Ambrose, Alice "Wittgenstein on Universals", *Metaphysics: Readings and Reappraisals,* ed. by W.E. Kennick etc., New Jersey, Prentice-Hall Inc. 1966, pp. 80-91.

Ammerman, R.R. "Wittgenstein's Later Methods", *Journal of Philosophy,* Vol. 58, 1961, pp. 707-708.

Anscombe, G.E.M. *An Introduction to Wittgenstein's Tractatus,* London, Hutchinson University Library, 1959.

Apel/Mohanty/Quinton "Discussion: Theories of Meaning in the Analytic and Continental Traditions", *Graduate faculty Philosophy Journal,* Vol. 7, 1978, pp. 79-105.

Ayer, A.J. "Phenomenalism", *Philosophical Essays,* A.J. Ayer, London, Macmillan, 1954, pp. 125-66.

Ayer, A.J. ed. by *The Revolution in Philosophy,* London, Macmillan, 1956.

Ayer, A.J. *The Concept of a Person and other Essays,* London, Macmillan, 1963.

Ayer, A.J. *Metaphysics and Commonsense,* London, Macmillan, 1967.

Ayer, A.J. and C. Taylor, ed. by "Symposium on Phenomenology and Linguistic Analysis", *Proceedings of the Aristotelian Society,* Sup. Vol. 33, 1959, pp. 93-124.

Bombrough, Renford "Universals and Family Resemblances", *Proceedings of the Aristotelian Society, Vol. 61,* 1960-61, pp. 207-22.

Bombrough, Renford — "Does Philosophy 'Leave everything as it is'? Even Theology?", *The Philosophy in Christianity* ed. by Godfrey Vesey. (*Supplement to* Philosophy *Magazine,* 1989).

Bernstein, Richard J. — "Wittgenstein's Three Languages", *Essays on Wittgenstein's Tractatus,* ed. by I.M. Copi, etc., London, Routledge and Kegan Paul Ltd. 1966, pp. 231-47.

Bhadra, M.K. — *Critical Survey of Phenomenology and Existentialism,* Allied Publisher, New Delhi, 1990.

Bird, Graham — *Philosophical Tasks : An Introduction to some Aims and Methods in Recent Philosophy,* London, Hutchinson University Library, 1972.

Black, Max — *A Companion to Wittgenstein's 'Tractarus',* Cambridge, Cambridge University Press, 1964.

Black, Max — "Some Problems Connected with Language", *Essays on Wittgenstein's Tractatus,* ed. by I.M. Copi etc., London, Routledge and Kegan Paul Ltd., 1966, pp. 183-203.

Boehm, R. — "Basic Reflections on Husserl's Phenomenological Reduction", *International Philosophical Quarterly,* Vol. 5, 1965, pp. 183-203.

Bogen, James — *Wittgenstein's Philosophy of Language,* London, Routledge and Kegan Paul, 1972.

Belton, Berek — *An Approach to Wittgenstein Philosophy,* London, Macmillan Press Ltd., 1979.

Burtt, E.A. — "Descriptive Metaphysics", *Mind,* Vol. 72, 1963, pp. 18-39.

Cairns, Dorion — "An Approach to Phenomenology", *Philosophical Essays in Memory of Edmund Husserl,* ed. by Marvin Farber, New York, The Philosophical Library, 1950, pp. 353-64.

Cairns, Dorion — "Phenomenology", *A History of Philosophical Systems,* ed. by V. Ferm, New York, The Philosophical Library, 1950, pp. 353-64.

Carr, David — *Phenomenology and problem of History,* Evanston, Northwestern University Press, 1974.

Carr, David — "Husserl's Problematic Concept of the Life-World", *Husserl: Expositions and Appraisals* ed. by Frederick A. Elliston etc., Notre Dame, University of Notre Dame Press, 1977.

Chappell, V.C. — "Ego and Person: Phenomenology or Analysis", *Monist,* Vol. 49, 1965, pp. 18-27.

Charlesworth, Maxwell John — *Philosophy and Linguistic Analysis,* (Duquesne Studies : Philosophical Series, 9), Pittsburgh, Duquesne University, 1959.

Chatterjee, Margaret — "Language as Phenomenon", *Philosophy and Phenomenological Research,* Vol. 30, 1969, pp. 116-21.

Chatterjee, Margaret — *The Existentialist Outlook,* New Delhi, Orient Longman, 1973.

Chaudhury, Pravas Jivan — "Describing and Prescribing : Philosophical Implications", *Philosophical Quarterly,* Vol. 8, 1958-59, pp. 273-79.

Cherry, Christopher — "Games and Language", *Mind,* Vol. 84, 1975 pp. 528-47.

Copi, I.M. — "Objects, Properties, Relations in the *Tractatus",* *Essays on Wittgenstein's Tractatus,* ed. by I.M. Copi etc., London, Routledge and Kegan Paul Ltd., 1966, pp. 167-86.

Cunningham, S. — *Language and the Phenomenological Reductions of Edmund Husserl,* The Hague, 1976.

DeBoer, Theodors — *The Development of Husserl's Thought* Eng. tr. by Theodore Plantinga, The Hague, 1976.

Delius, Marald — "Descriptive Interpretation", *Philosophy and Phenomenological Research,* Vol. 13, 1953, pp. 305-23.

Dellon, M.C. — "Special Contribution to the Debate : Theoria, Praxis and the Crisis", *Analecta Husserliana* (The year book of Phenomenological Research) Vol. 5, ed. by Anna-Teresa Tymieniecka, U.S.A., Reidel Publishing Company 1976, pp. 179-83.

Drury, M. O'C — "A Symposium : Assessments on the Man and the Philosophers", *The Man and his Philosophy,* ed. by K.T. Fann, New Jersey : Humanities Press, 1967.

Durfee, H.A. — *Introduction to Analytic Philosophy and Phenomenology,* ed. by H.A. Durfee, The Hague, 1976, pp. 1-13.

Edie, James M. — *Speaking and Meaning : The Phenomenology of Language,* London, Indiana University Press, 1976.

Edie, James M. — "Phenomenology as a Rigorous science", *International Philosophical Quarterly,* Vol. 7, 1967, pp. 21-30.

Embree, Lester E — "An Interpretation of the doctrine of the Ego in Husserl's *Ideen", Phenomenology : Continuation and Criticism,* ed. by F. Kersten etc., The Hague, 1973, pp. 24-32.

Farber, M — "The Ideal of a Presuppositionless Philosophy", *Philosophical Essays in Memory of Edmund Husserl,* ed. by M. Farber, Greenwood Press Publishers, New Delhi, 1965, pp. 44-64.

Farber, M. — *Philosophy and Existence,* New York, Harber and Torchbooks, 1967.

Farber, M. — *The Aims of Phenomenology : The Motives, Methods, and Impact of Husserl's Thought,* New York, Harper and Torchbooks 1966.

Feyerabend, Paul — "Wittgenstein's Philosophical Investigations", *Wittgenstein : The Philosophical Investigations* (A Collection of Critical Essays), ed. by G. Pitcher, London, Univesity of Notre Dame Press, 1968.

Finch, Henry Le Roy — *Wittgenstein's Early Philosophy : An Exposition of the Tractatus,* New York, Humanities Press, 1971.

Finch, Henry Le Roy — *Wittgenstein's Later Philosophy : An Exposition of the Philosophical Investigations,* New Jersey, Humanities Press, 1977.

Findlay, J.N. — "Phenomenology", *Encyclopedia Brittannica,* Vol. 17, 1963.

Flew, Antony — "Philosophy and Language", *Essays in Conceptual Analysis,* ed. by Antony Flew, London, Macmillan, 1956, pp. 1-20.

Gahringer, R.E. "Can Games Explain Language?", *Journal of Philosophy,* Vol. 56, 1959, pp. 661-67.

Gendlin, Eugene T. "What are the Grounds of Explications ? A Basic Problem in Linguistic Analysis and in Phenomenology", *Monist,* Vol. 49, 1965, pp. 137-64.

Gellner, Ernest *Words and Things,* London, Bosten Beacon Press, 1960.

Gregorios, Paulos Mar "Phenomenology and the Transcendent : Which way Does one Transcend ?" Presented for ICPR/ CARP Conference on Phenomenology and Indian Philosophy, New Delhi, 1988.

Griffin, James *Wittgenstein's Logical Atomism,* London, Oxford University Press, 1964.

Gruender, David "Wittgenstein on Explanation and Description", *Journal of Philosophy,* Vol. 59, 1962, pp. 523-30.

Gurwitsch, Aron "Problem of the Life-World", *Phenomenology and Social Reality,* ed. by Maurice Natanson, The Hague, 1970, pp. 35-61.

Hamilton, Kenneth G. "Edmund Husserl's Contribution to Philosophy", *Journal of Philosophy,* Vol. 36, 1939, pp. 225- 32.

Heekan, Patrick A. "Experiment and the Fulfilment of Theory", presented for ICPR/CARP Conference on Phenomenology and Indian Philosophy, New Delhi 1988.

Heidegger, Martin *Being and Time,* Eng. tr. of *Sein Und Zeit* by John Macquarrie and Edward Robinson, Oxford, Basil Blackwell, 1962.

Hem, John M. "Husserl and/or Wittgenstein", *International Philosophical Quarterly,* Vol. 8, 1968, pp. 547-78.

Hervey, Helen "The Problem of the Model Language Game in Wittgenstein's Later Philosophy", *Philosophy,* Vol. 36, 1961, pp. 333-51.

Hester, Marcus B *The Meaning of Poetic Metaphor,* The Hague, Mouton and Co., 1967.

Hochberg, Herbert "Material Properties in the *Tractatus", Essays on Wittgenstein,* ed. by E.D. Klemke, Chicago, University of Illinois Press, 1971, pp. 120-200.

Husserl, Edmund — *Phenomenology as Rigorous Science,* Eng. tr. by Quentin Lauer, *Edmund Husserl : Phenomenology and the Crisis of Philosophy,* New York, Harper Torchbooks, 1965.

Husserl, Edmund — *Ideas : General Introduction to Pure Phenomenology,* Eng. tr. by W.R. Gibson, New York, Humanities Press Inc., 1952.

Husserl, Edmund — *The Idea of Phenomenology,* Eng. tr. by W.P. Alston and G. Nakhnikian, The Hague, 1964.

Husserl, Edmund — *Cartesian Meditations : An Introduction to Phenomenology,* Eng. tr. by Dorion Cairns, The Hague, 1977.

Ihde, Don — "Some parallels - between Analysis and Phenomenology", *Philosophical and Phenomenological Research,* Vol. 27, 1967, pp. 577-86.

Kaufmann, Felix — "Phenomenology and Logical Empiricism", *Philosophical Essays in Memory of Edmund Husserl,* ed. by Marvin Farber, pp. 124-42.

Kersten, F. — "The Occassion and Novelty of Husserl's Phenomenology of Essence", *Phenomenological Perspectives,* (ed), Herbert Spiegelberg. The Hague, 1975, pp. 61-92.

Kersten, F. — "Husserl's Doctrine of Noesis Noema", *Phenomenology : Continuation and Criticism,* ed. by F. Kersten etc., The Hague, 1973, pp. 114-44.

Klemke, E.D. — "The Ontology of Wittgenstein's *Tractatus", Essays on Wittgenstein,* ed. by E.D. Klemke, Chicago, University of Illinois Press, 1971, pp. 104-19.

Keyt, David — "Wittgenstein's notion of an object", *Essays on Wittgenstein's Tractatus,* ed. by I.M. Copi etc., London, Routledge and Kegan Paul Ltd., 1966, pp. 289-303.

Kuntz, Paul Grimley — "Order in Language, Phenomena and Reality : Notes on Linguistic Analysis, Phenomenology and Metaphysics", *Monist,* Vol. 49, 1965, pp. 107-36.

Landgrebe, Ludwig — "The Phenomenological Concept of Experience", *Philosophy and Phenomenological Research,* Vol. 34, 1973-74, pp. 1-13.

Landgrebe, Ludwig — "Phenomenology and Metaphysics", *Philosophy and Phenomenological Research,* Vol. 10, 1940, pp. 197-205.

Lauer, Quentin — *Phenomenology : Its genesis and prospect,* New York, Harper Torchbooks, 1958.

Locke, John — *An Essay Concerning Human Understanding,* abridged and edited. by A.D. Woozley, Great Britain, Fontana Library, 1964.

MacNabb, D.G.C. — "David Hume", *Encyclopedia of Philosophy,* ed. by Paul Edwards, Vol. 4, London, Macmillan, 1967, pp. 74-90.

Malcolm, N — "Wittgenstein's Philosophical Investigations", *Philosophical Review,* Vol. 63, 1954, pp. 530-59.

Malcolm, N. — "The Book Review of *English Philosophy since 1900",* G.J. Warnock, London, 1968, *The Philosophical Review,* Vol. 68, 1959, pp. 256-58.

Malcolm, N. — Ludwig Wittgenstein : A Memior, (Revised edition), London, Oxford University Press, 1966.

Mall, R.A. — *Experience and Reason : The Phenomenology of Husserl and its Relation to Hume's Philosophy,* The Hague, 1973.

Mall, R.A. — "Phenomenology – Essentialistic or Descriptive?", presented for ICPR/CARP, Conference, Phenomenology, and Indian Philosophy, New Delhi 1988.

Manser, Anthony — "Games and Family Resemblances", *Philosophy,* Vol. 42, 1967, pp. 210-25.

McDougall, Derek A — "'Descriptive' and 'Revisionary' Metaphysics", *Philosophy and Phenomenological Research,* Vol. 34, 1973-74, pp. 209-23.

McGill, V.J. — "Evidence in Husserl's Phenomenology", *Phenomenology : Continuation and Criticism,* ed. by F. Kersten etc., The Hague, 1973, pp. 145-66.

McGuinness, B.F. — "Pictures and Form in Wittgenstein's *'Tractatus'*", *Essays on Wittgenstein's Tractatus,* ed. by I.M. Copi etc., London, Routledge and Kegan Paul Ltd., 1966, pp. 127-56.

Mizuno, Kazuhisa — "The Paradox of the Phenomenological Method", *Analecta Husserliana,* (The yearbook of Phenomenological Research), Vol. VIII, Y. Nitta and H. Tatematsu, Holland, D. Reidel Publishing Company, 1979, pp. 37-53.

Mohanty, J.N. — "Individual Fact and Essence in Edmund Husserl's Philosophy", *Philosophy and Phenomenological Research* Vol. 20, 1959-60, pp. 222-30.

Mohanty, J.N. — "Philosophical Description", *Philosophical Papers, First Series,* ed. by Kalidas Bhattacharyya, Visva Bharti, Santiniketan, 1969, pp. 1-18.

Mohanty, J.N. — "Phenomenology and Ontology", *Phenomenology and Ontology,* ed. by J.N. Mohanty, The Hague, 1970, pp. 92-103.

Mohanty, J.N. — "The Given", *Phenomenology and Ontology,* ed. by J.N. Mohanty, The Hague 1970, pp. 12-21.

Mohanty, J.N. — "'Life-World' and 'A Priori' in Husserl's Later Thought", *Analecta Husserliana,* Vol. III, 1974, ed. by Anna-Teresa, Tymieniecka, Holland, D. Reidel Publishing Company pp. 46-65.

Mohanty, J.N. — *Husserl's Theory of Meaning,* (Third Edition), The Hague, 1976.

Mohanty, J.N. — "Husserl's Transcendental Phenomenology and Essentialism", *Metaphysics,* Vol. 32, 1978, pp. 299-321.

Mohnty, J.N. — *The Possibility of Transcendental Philosophy,* Boston, 1985.

Mohanty, J.N. — "Philosophical Description", *Research in Phenomenology,* Vol. XIV, 1987.

Molina, Fernando — "The Husserlian Ideal of a Pure Phenomenology", *An Invitation to Phenomenology,* ed. by James M. Edie, Chicago, Quadrangle Books, 1965, pp. 161-79.

Mundle, C.N.E. — *Critique of Linguistic Philosophy,* Oxford, Clarendon Press, 1981.

Munitz, Milton Karl, — *Contemporary Analytic Philosophy,* Macmillan, New Delhi, 1981.

Murált, Andréde	*The Idea of Phenomenology, Husserlian Exemplarism,* Eng. tr. by Garry L. Breckon, Evanston, Northwestern University Press, 1974.
Natanson, Maurice	"Phenomenology and the Natural Attitude", *Journal of Philosophy,* Vol. 56, 1959, p. 965.
Natanson, Maurice	"Phenomenology as a Rigorous Science", *International Philosophical Quarterly,* Vol. VII, 1967, pp. 5-20.
O'Connor, D.J.	"Locke", *A Critical History of Western Philosophy,* ed. by D.J. O'Connor, New York, The Free Press, Macmillan, 1964, pp. 204-19.
Orth/Trier, Ernst Wolfhang	"Unity and Plurality of cultures in the perspectives of Edmund Husserl and Ernst Carrlrer", presented for ICPR/CARP conference on Phenomenology and Indian Philosophy, New Delhi 1988.
Pappe, H.O.	"Philosophical Anthropology", *Encyclopedia of Philosophy,* ed. by Edwards Paul, Vol. 6, 1967, pp. 159-66.
Patocka, Jean	"The Husserlian Doctrine of Eidetic Instuition and Its Recent Critics", *Husserl : Expositions and appraisals,* ed. by Frederick, A. Elliston etc., 1977, pp. 150-59.
Paul, G.A.	"Wittgenstein", *The Revolution in Philosophy,* ed. by A.J. Ayer etc., London, Macmillan, 1956, pp. 88-96.
Pears, David	"*Wittgenstein,* Great Britain, Fontana, 1971.
Pepper, Stephen C	*World Hypotheses, A study in Evidence,* Berkeley, University of California Press, 1942.
Pettit, Philip	"On Phenomenology as a Methodology of Philosophy", *Linguistic Analysis and Phenomenology,* ed. by W. Mays and Brown, Lewisburg : Bucknell University Press.
Peursen, C.A. Van	"Edmund Husserl and Ludwig Wittgenstein", *Philosophy and Phenomenological Research,* Vol. 20, 1959, pp. 181-97.
Peursen, C.A. Van	*Ludwig Wittgenstein,* Eng. tr. by Rex Ambler, London, Faber and Faber, 1969.

Peursen, C.A. Van — *Phenomenology and Analytical Philosophy,* Pittsburgh, Pa, Duquesne University Press, 1972.

Pivcevic, Edo — *Husserl and Phenomenology* London, Hutchinson University Library, 1970.

Pivcevic, Edo — "Concepts, Phenomenology and Philosophical Understanding", *Phenomenology and Philosophical Understanding,* ed. by Edo Pivcevic, Cambridge, Cambridge University Press, 1975, pp. 271-86.

Polanyi, M — *Personal Knowledge : Towards A Post Critical Philosophy,* Chicago, The University of Chicago Press, 1958.

Pole, David — *The Later Philosophy of Wittgenstein,* London, Athlane Press, 1958.

Pompa, L — "Family Resemblance", *Philosophical Quarterly,* Vol. 17, 1967, pp. 63-69.

Putman, Hilary — *Mind, Language and Reality, Philosophical Papers,* Vol. 2, Cambridge University Press, Cambridge, 1975.

Raval, R.K. — "An Essay on 'Phenomenology'" , *Philosophy and Phenomenological Research,* Vol. 33, 1973, pp. 216-26.

Rajan, R. Sundara — *Studies in Phenomenology and Deconstruction,* ICPR, New Delhi, 1991.

Rajan, R. Sundara — "Nature and Life World : Towards a Hermeneutics of Nature", presented for ICPR/CARP Conference on Phenomenology and Indian Philosophy, New Delhi, 1988.

Rescher, Nicholas — "Translation As A Tool of Philosophical Analysis", *Journal of Philosophy,* Vol. 53, 1956, pp. 219-24.

Ricoeur, P. — *Husserl : An Analysis of his Phenomenology,* Eng. tr. and ed. by G. Ballard and Lester E. Embree, Evanston, Northwestern University Press, 1967.

Rhees, Rush — "Wittgenstein's 'Builder's'", *Proceeding of the Aristotelian Society,* Vol. 60, 1959-60, pp. 171-86.

Rhees, Rush — "Preface to *The Blue and Brown Books",* L. Wittgenstein, Oxford, Basil Blackwell, 1958.

Rickman, H.P. "Wilhelm Dilthey", *Encyclopedia of Philosophy,* ed. by Paul Edwards, Vol. 2, 1967, pp. 403-407.

Rosenberg, Jay F. "Wittgenstein's Theory of Language As Picture", *American Philosophical Quarterly,* Vol. 5, 1968, pp. 18-30.

Rosenberg, Jay F. *Linguistic Representation,* U.S.A., Publishing Company, 1974.

Runciman, W.G. "Describing", *Mind,* Vol. LXXXI, July, 1972.

Russell, B. *Human Knolwdge : Its Scope and Limits,* London, Allen and Unwin, 1948.

Russell, B. *Our Knowledge of the External World,* New York, (A Mentor Book) New American Library, 1960.

Ryle, G. "The Theory of Meaning", *British Philosophy in the Mid-Century,* ed. by M.C. Mace, London, Allen and Unwin, 1957.

Ryle, G. "Ordinary Language", *Ordinary Language,* ed. by V.C. Chappell, New Jersey, Prentice-Hall, 1964, pp. 24-40.

Salman, C.V. "The Starting Point of Husserl's Philosophy *Proceedings of the Aristotelian Society,* Vol. 30, 1929-30, pp. 55-78.

Schmit, Richard "Husserl's Transcendental Phenomenological Reduction", *Philosophy and Phenomenological Research,* Vol. 20, 1959-60, pp. 238-45.

Schmit, Richard "Phenomenology and Metaphysics", *Journal of Philosophy,* Vol. 59, 1962, pp. 421-28.

Schmit, Richard "Phenomenology and Analysis", *Philosophy and Phenomenological Research,* Vol. 23, 1962-63, pp. 101-10.

Schmit, Richard "Phenomenology", *Encyclopedia of Philosophy,* Vol. 6, ed. by Paul Edwards, New York, 1967.

Schwyzer, H.R.G. "Wittgenstein's Picture Theory of Language", *Inquiry,* Vol. 5, 1962, pp. 46-63.

Schwyzer, H.R.G. "Naming and Saying", *Essays on Wittgenstein's Tractatus,* ed. by I.M. Copi, etc., London, Routledge and Kegan Paul Ltd., 1966, pp. 240- 71.

Seebohm, Thomas M. "The Paradox of Subjectivity and the Idea of Ultimate Grounding in Husserl and Heidegger", presented for ICPR/CARP Conference on Phenomenology and Indian Philosophy, New Delhi, 1988.

Shimomisse, Elichi "Philosophy and Phenomenological Institution", *Analecta Husserliana,* Vol. VIII, ed. by Nitta and H. Tatamatsu, U.S.A., D. Reidel Publishing Company, 1979, pp. 63-77.

Smart, Harold R. "Language-Games", *Philosophical Quarterly,* Vol. 7, 1957, pp. 224-35.

Solomon, Robert C. *From Rationalism to Existentialism,* New York, Harper and Row, 1972.

Spiegelberg, H. "On Some Human Uses of Phenomenology", *Phenomenology in Perspective,* ed. by F.J. Smith, The Hague, 1970, pp. 16-31.

Spiegelberg, H. "Husserl's Way into Phenomenology for Americans: A Letter and its Sequel", *Phenomenology: Continuation and Criticism,* ed. by F. Kersten etc., The Hague, 1973, pp. 168-91.

Spiegelberg, H. "How Subjective is Phenomenology?", *Doing Phenomenology, : Essays on and in Phenomenology,* ed. by H. Spiegelberg, The Hegue, 1975.

Spiegelberg, H. *Phenomenological Movement : A Historical Introduction,* (Second Edition), Vol. I, The Hague, 1976.

Stegmüller, W. *Main Currents in Contemporary German, British and American Philosophy,* Eng. tr. by Albert E. Blumberg, 4th edition, Holland, D. Reidel Publishing Company, 1969.

Strawson. P.F. *Individuals,* London, Methuen, 1959.

Sweeney Robert D. "Affectivity and the Life World", *Analecta Husserliana,* Vol. V. ed. by Anne-Teresa Tymieniecka, Holland, D. Reidel Publishing Company, 1976, pp. 71-82.

TeHennepe, Eugene — "The Life-World and the World of Ordinary Language", *An Invitation to Phenomenology,* edited with introduction, James M. Edie, Chicago, Quadrangle Books, 1965, pp. 134-46.

Tillman, Frank — "Phenomenological and Philosophical Analysis", *International Philosophical Quarterly,* Vol. 6, 1966, pp. 465-82.

Tillman, Frank — "Transcendental Phenomenology and Analytic Philosophy", *International Philosophical Quarterly.* Vol. VII, 1967, pp. 31-40.

Tugendhat, Erndt — "Phenomenology and Linguistic Analysis", *Husserl: Expositions and for Appraisals* ed. by Frederick A. Ellistan etc., pp. 325-57.

Tugendhat, Erndt — "Description as Method of Philosophy : A Reply to Mr. Pettit", *Linguistic Analysis and Phenomenology,* ed. by W. May and Brown, Lewishburg : Bucknell University Press, Great Britain, 1969.

Urmson, J.O. — *Philosophical Analysis,* London : Oxford University Press, Paperback edition, 1967.

Waismann, F. — "How I See Philosophy", *How I See Philosophy,* ed. by R. Harre, London, Macmillan, 1968, pp. 1-38.

Warnock, G.J. — *English Philosophy Since 1900,* London, Oxford University Press, paperback, 1966.

Warnock, Mary — *Existentialism,* London, Oxford University Press, 1970.

Weissman, David — "Ontology in the *Tractatus", Philosophy and Phenomenological Research,* Vol. 27, 1967, pp. 475-501.

Weitz, Morris — "Philosophical Analysis", *Encyclopedia of Philosophy,* Vol. I, ed. by Edward Paul, London, Macmillan, 1967, pp. 97-105.

Werkmeister, W.H. — "On 'Describing a World'", *Philosophy and Phenomenological Research,* Vol. 11, 1950, pp. 303-25.

Wild, John — "Is There a World of Ordinary Language?", *Philosophical Review,* Vol. 67, 1958, pp. 460-76.

Index